Getting

or

Bitter

....

Getting

Better

Getting Bitter *or* Getting Better

Choosing forgiveness for your own good

by David W. Schell, Ed.D.

Cover Design:
Scott Wannemuehler

Library of Congress Catalog Number
90-85280

ISBN 0-87029-231-5

Contents

LIST OF FIGURES

Introduction

Hate poisons; forgiveness heals. It's that simple—or is it? Why not end this book here, use this ancient truth, and begin growing into loving, mature, warm human beings? What a beautiful idea, but in real life we must deal with the fact that we are, indeed, human beings.

Human hatred knows no bounds. In his book, *The Nazi Doctors,* Robert Jay Lifton struggled with "...the disturbing psychological truth that ... ordinary people can commit demonic acts." [1] The propensity for hurtful behavior is a malignancy which infects to the point of risking world destruction and can crush the most cherished relationship.

A garden variety example from the daily newspaper illustrates common bitterness:

DEADLY REJECTION

Miami (AP)—A leukemia victim's long-lost brother has rejected pleas to determine whether his bone marrow is compatible, dashing the patient's best hope for survival.

"If he dies, he dies. He's about as much a brother to me as you are," Randy Jeff C. told a reporter for *The Miami News.*

C., 31, lives on the street here, working as a test subject for medical experiments. He refused to undergo tests that would check if he could donate marrow to his brother. C. has another brother and a sister whohave already been tested and found incompatible.[2]

Compare his attitude with a woman who had every right to hate, but somehow chose a better way:

1

A woman, misdiagnosed and kept in a state mental hospital for seventeen years, has returned in triumph to the institution as a full-time administrator after earning a master's degree from Harvard.

Marie Balter was seventeen and clinically depressed when she was labeled schizophrenic and sent to Danvers State Hospital. After gaining her release in 1964, she went back to school and has since worked with psychiatric patients, lectured nationwide, and written an autobiography. Her story was the basis of a 1986 TV movie starring Marlo Thomas.

"I wouldn't have grown one bit if I hadn't learned to forgive," she said in an interview. "If you don't forgive your parents or your children or yourself, you don't get beyond that anger.

"Forgiving is a way of reaching out from a bad past and heading out to a more positive future."[3]

There is no known cure for being human. But we can act better. Human beings have the capacity for love, healing, and growth.

Psychotherapy is one process of getting better. The word is a combination of two ancient Greek words, *psyche*, referring to the air or spirit in a person, and *therapeia*, meaning to heal. Literally, psychotherapy means to heal the spirit.

A psychotherapist—commonly referred to as a therapist—may point out roadblocks which impede progress and stunt personal development. A therapist may provide guidance, support, insight, encouragement, and even confrontation. In the final analysis, however, we are responsible for our own choices. No therapist, no book, no law can force us to make changes we do not want to make.

Yet, because we can and do make choices, we have hope. Feeling unable to make choices about our psychological or emotional wellbeing makes life seem out of control. Indeed, it is out of control when we fail to take responsibility for making choices that either cripple us or contribute to our growth. This book will focus on some of the most important choices we will ever make. These choices are so life-changing that they may even affect our children for generations to come. Most of all, when we bring life under control by our choices, we are no longer willing to allow others to dictate our emotional health in counterproductive ways.

Therapeutic forgiveness is such a healing dynamic that I wonder why it is so commonly overlooked. Those of us in professional practice focus on preparation, degrees, certifications, licensures, and continuing education. But I have never had a course on forgiveness. I have studied more than a hundred therapeutic modalities, but the use of forgiveness has not been one of them. Professionals have written volumes on diagnosis and treatment, yet there is very little on understanding the need to forgive and to put this potent force to work in our lives.

Relegating forgiveness to the domain of religion, psychotherapists rarely incorporate it into clinical practice and, unfortunately, only a few spiritual leaders appreciate its psychotherapeutic value. The personal discovery and exercise of therapeutic forgiveness, then, may be a lonely, largely unexplored one.

But take heart; therapeutic forgiveness does work! That is what really counts. People who have suffered the malignancy of fermented hostility have made remarkable recoveries. So can you.

My approach to forgiveness draws from clinical psychotherapeutic practice and the Judeo-Christian tradition. No doubt this will offend purists in each camp. Nevertheless, I will draw from the best and likely desecrate a few sacred cows and smash a few icons. Although I cannot find it in my heart to apologize, perhaps you will find it in yours to forgive.

Internalized hatred is not always the other person's problem and, while it is universal, some suffer more than others. Those who see no need to forgive are particularly unfortunate. I will touch more on that later. I sincerely wish you had no need for this book, but deep inside when you've laid aside all defenses, you and I will recognize an alarming need for healing forgiveness.

Most of my discoveries about the power of therapeutic forgiveness developed during fifteen years of clinical practice. I have come to love and respect many wonderful people as we walked together through the debris of human tragedy on the way to healthy living. These people taught me much, and throughout this book I will illustrate truths and dynamics I discovered as they opened their lives and shared their thoughts and feelings. In each instance, I change details to protect identity and sometimes construct a representative picture with elements from several cases. I will also preserve clinical integrity. I am grateful to colleagues who have shared numerous case histories with me.

I have been associated with children during much of my career. Many have every right to hate and are hell-bent on destroying their lives to express that hatred. Children have more difficulty recognizing their need to forgive, but they are more forgiving when they finally understand that need. Children are marvelous teachers.

Every parent makes mistakes—serious ones—and no person grows into adulthood without a need to forgive their parents. Perhaps Oscar Wilde said it best in *The Picture of Dorian Gray*: "Children begin by loving their parents; as they grow older they judge them; sometimes they forgive them."[4]

By their encouragement, my professional associates have moved me deeply. But one need not be a professional to make healing changes. A year ago I had a brief conversation with a woman who understood very little psychological jargon. Now I have a letter from her telling me how she has salvaged her life and family by taking a serious journey into the seemingly impossible labyrinth of forgiveness.

Forgiveness is fascinating, but many people put up immediate defenses, conjuring up every possible excuse to explain why the need to forgive is not relevant to them. If you are in this category, relax; it is a normal reaction. C.S. Lewis summarized, "Everyone says forgiveness is a lovely idea until they have something to forgive..."[5] No one can force you to forgive anyone or anything. The choice will always be yours.

While growing up, I heard many sermons and lessons on forgiveness, but the emphasis was usually on my sins and my need to be forgiven. I have no quarrel with that, but what about me when I am the victim! At least it is refreshing to focus on the wrongdoing of others.

In the field of therapy, the personality of the therapist is a major tool. Therapy is filtered through the personality of the therapist, and the same is true of forgiveness. It must permeate one's personality. Therapists who are chronically bitter are not likely to find forgiveness very helpful in life or practice. But when one discovers therapeutic forgiveness as a means to get better, professional skills are apt to improve significantly. Therapeutic forgiveness is contagious.

What is true for psychotherapists, of course, is true for everyone. We present a personality to the world; it is how we see ourselves and how others see us from first impressions to the lasting impact we make on those we love. Personality, when allowed to ferment in anger and hostility, becomes malignant and bitter. Psychotherapeutic forgiveness offers hope. As we get better, we become more therapeutic people.

Chapter One, "Resistance to Therapeutic Forgiveness," begins where most of us start, with emphasis on resistance. The fact that you opened this book, much less read this far, may indicate that you are a special breed. The chapter explores basic misconceptions, common roadblocks, along with the hurt and anger of victimization. This takes special courage, but you are a special person.

Chapter Two deals with "Recognizing the Need to Forgive." It begins with a journey into ourselves. It is easier to overlook or bury the need to forgive than to face ourselves. Early lessons on reality distortion (we usually learn this well), will focus on self-appraisal, damage control, and assuming responsibility for our real feelings. While the journey is not like a trip to Disneyland, everyone should make it at least once.

Chapter Three, "Beginning with Self-Forgiveness," gets even more personal and we should begin feeling better. We will examine damaged self-esteem, needless guilt, and poor emotional hygiene. We will learn to love ourselves. The journey may get complicated, but if Dorothy and Toto could find their way back to Kansas, we will find our way, too.

Chapter Four, "Becoming a Forgiving Person," gets down to some nuts and bolts of "how to." We will survey ways to focus on specific villains, control anger, and get over the mountain. Still a long way from home, we will at least have the wind blowing in the right direction. Columbus must have had similar feelings.

Chapter Five, "Forgiving, Healing and Growing," heads us down the home stretch. In this chapter we investigate the possibility of having forgiveness fail (yes, this side trip is really necessary), forgiving the unforgivable, and aspiring to the major leagues. Our journey together ends there. But since life is what you make it, your saga into personal forgiveness, healing, and growth will have only just begun.

Finally, every book should have a conclusion. But the effect of therapeutic forgiveness in your life will be the only conclusion that really matters.

CHAPTER I

Resistance to Therapeutic Forgiveness

"Maybe if I hate enough I'll be happy." While this attitude does not make sense, nonetheless, many fear that giving it up will separate them forever from their hope for happiness. But before becoming too critical, we should understand that resisting therapeutic forgiveness is a normal protective mechanism which takes subtle and obvious forms. Usually your resistance is more obvious to me, and mine, of course, is more obvious to you.

While some resistance mechanisms may be more valid than others, the common denominator for all forms of resistance is that they block healing and growing. Yet, we acquire mechanisms for good reasons. The main reason is survival, not necessarily physical but certainly emotional. We usually adopt mechanisms in the early developmental years of life to help meet basic needs. In infancy, crying and frowning brought milk a little faster. Later, we used temper tantrums to register demands in a powerful, adult-dominated world. Unfortunately, these mechanisms do not work in later life, but we perceive the need to hold on to frustration, anger, and hostility. Forgiveness is threatening; it challenges the power of these negative and destructive emotional forces.

Therapeutic forgiveness may appear to defy our best efforts to control ourselves and those around us. It can break down barriers and make us vulnerable to those who might use and abuse us. Worse yet, others may perceive it as weakness.

Even considering deep forgiveness requires a healthy dose of bravery. But it is an adventure. At any rate, internal resistance may handicap our best efforts and allow us to avoid the issue altogether.

How one resists forgiveness is unique to the individual, but the more common forms of resistance are identifiable and close to our own.

SOME BASIC MISCONCEPTIONS
"But I don't want to love that awful person."

Loss of power

Most of us feel we have little or no control over our lives and that our lives are over-regulated. Recently, on a visit through a beautiful southern park, I became aware of so many negative signs. "No" and "Do Not" appeared over and over. One sign even said, "Do not molest the alligators!" I have encountered many forms of perversion, but I wondered what kind of rare bestiality had disturbed the park officials.

Realistically, few of us control our communities, jobs, or taxes. We may, perhaps, have a marginal control of our families, but divorce, reported abuse, and the ever-increasing power of growing children limit even this control.

Laws, social customs, financial realities, and conditioning regulate our lives. Prisons and mental hospitals are filled with people who trespass these boundaries.

Understandably, we seek a few areas of life we can control. These areas affirm our autonomy and the control makes us feel like real people.

We tend to equate hate with strength and love with weakness. We become vulnerable with too much love while hate, on the other hand, offers a sense of self-protection. It serves to keep others at bay. We perceive forgiveness as "wimpish," but those who can forgive find untold strength of character.

I cannot make anyone love me. I might love them, but they may not return that love. In a light-hearted tone, but with a note of developed self-esteem, I often say, "I am one of the nicest people I know." Of course, some people dislike me and a few even hate me, but they usually have other problems, too. Later, I will say more on learning to like ourselves and how to build self-esteem. When others do not love me, I feel powerless. Although I'm really not, I still feel that way. I do not have control.

Personal bitterness is different. It is controllable. Harboring hatred gives the illusion of maintaining control over those who have abused us and gives hope for vengeance. With enough resentment and guilt, the offender will surely change. This is a delusion, of course, but it gives a sense of power over those who crush us. Hate is so easy.

The idea of mystical power emerging from thoughts and feelings has a long tradition. The ancient Hebrews provided the foundations for the Judeo-Christian influence of our culture. They believed that certain verbal pronouncements released powers to accomplish the spoken word. Such pronouncements could be a blessing as well as a curse, but after the word was spoken, one could not recall the power.

I was five years old when I learned how this tradition affects modern life. My four-year-old brother stepped on my toy car, evoking a loud and clear "Damn you!" from me. The power of my curse boomeranged in full force to the seat of my pants.

We cannot control the behavior of other people, but we can withhold forgiveness, believing that our hostility will intimidate them. Unwittingly, our attempt to control others by hating robs us of self-control. Our own bitterness becomes our adversary.

Another illusion of power that non-forgiveness fosters is the need to put down offenders. Forgiveness demands that we relinquish the delusion of moral superiority, but we don't want to forfeit our right to complain, belittle, and attack. Forgiveness strips us of the satisfaction we gain by demeaning others and lording it over them. It is natural to want the power to knock others down; it is not natural to pick up the gauntlet of personal growth and loving compassion.

Abuse viewed as love

Children often confuse love and abuse when those who are supposed to love them abuse them. Unfortunately, some of these children grow into adults who abuse others or subject themselves to further abuse in adult life. Eighty-five to ninety percent of those in state prisons were victimized as children. Others find themselves involved in a succession of self-destructive domestic relationships.

Therapists are beginning to recognize that, indeed, there are persons caught in the web of self-defeating patterns of behavior. It is becoming recognized as an identifiable syndrome far more common than those whose lives are shattered by it ever imagined. At last it has a name—self-defeating personality.

Everyone suffers some self-defeating characteristics; a few are handicapped so severely that they are unable to respond to caring, emotional warmth, and commitment.

A common example is a wife who is beaten over and over. Police are frustrated when battered women file charges only to drop those charges or bail the abuser out of jail within forty-eight hours. Some officers amuse themselves by making bets on how long it will take the victim to rescue the perpetrator.

Some of these women, battered so severely, may finally end the relationship. Unfortunately, many will often return to the relationship or find another abuser who takes up where the first one left off. A few die. Abuse and love somehow become synonymous.

As children, most of us experienced guilt and eventually confessed so we could be punished and feel better. It worked in childhood, but it can be devastating in adult life. The misperception is that if we forgive we must let go of the self-punishing behaviors we have always hoped would make us feel better.

Occasionally, unforgiveness is a mechanism for keeping a sick, self-punishing relationship alive. Therapeutic forgiveness separates abuse and love. No one needs to be subjected to hurt as the price for love. Abuse produces victims; love generates growth.

Irrational ideas

Early in my career, I worked on an inpatient alcohol detoxification and rehabilitation ward where I learned much about life. I still repeat the Prayer of Serenity and find it helpful for personal growth.

Alcoholics tend to be remarkable people and I've known only a few I did not like as individuals. They frequently have emotional insights, are good communicators, and intelligent—if only alcoholism didn't leave such a trail of human debris. Yet that is what addiction is all about.

I am often reminded of a maxim we used on the rehabilitation ward: "It's the stinkin' thinkin' that causes the drinkin'." No one is sure who coined the phrase, but the truth is that "stinkin' thinkin' " causes much more than drinking. It accounts for a great deal of misery and is particularly relevant to an unwillingness to forgive.

In my work with children, I meet scores of hardcore delinquents. They are not stupid youngsters; actually, they do stupid things because they are angry. For whatever reason, they are steeped in an anger that ferments into such hostility that it overrides their brains. Never have I known a teenager addicted to drugs who was not an expert on the dangers of abuse.

We will not have unusual success with delinquent teenagers until we find a way to help them straighten out their thinking and learn to forgive. I often ask tough, macho young men if they like girls. This usually gets a strong reaction since it seems to imply they are homosexual. I follow that with another question. "Why, then, do you continue to do things that get you locked up with boys? It simply doesn't make sense if you really prefer to be with girls."

When I work with these delinquent and predelinquent kids, I sometimes refer to their behavior as "thinking with your butt." We discuss the difference between thinking with one's behind versus one's brain. With a little guidance, an unusually hardened thirteen year old made this discovery:

> I had my butt and brains turned around. My butt is not too smart, my brains are made to think. But I've been thinking with my butt and shitting with my brains.

Indeed he had. Freud could not have analyzed it more accurately. Fortunately, this young man was able to put his brain in gear. He realized the damage his hatred was creating for himself, forgave major hurts, and began building a productive life. It was not a surprise when his grades began to improve.

Certain assumptions establish the premise that rational thinking is of therapeutic value. More directly, Albert Ellis developed a therapeutic system based on what he termed a "rational emotive approach." With unusual insight, Dr. Ellis formulated a list of common irrational assumptions which impair rational thinking. Several items in his list have particular value for clearing up misconceptions which restrict forgiveness:

- The idea that certain people are bad, wicked, or villainous, and that they should be punished for their villainy.
- The idea that it is awful and catastrophic when things are not the way one would like them to be.
- The idea that human unhappiness is caused externally and that people have little or no ability to control their terrors and disturbances.

- The idea that it is easier to avoid than to face life's difficulties and self responsibilities.
- The idea that one's past history is an all-important determiner of one's present behavior and that because something once strongly affected one's life, it should affect it indefinitely.[1]

While rational thinking and forgiveness are not the same, reasoning helps us through the maze of our own "stinkin' thinkin'. " In short, nonforgiveness is irrational. We hurt only ourselves; it has no effect on those who violate us. We are weakened, not strengthened, by our own emotional cancer. Rational thinking helps us make forgiving choices.

Dread of reconciliation

Does forgiveness mean we must love someone we now hate? Few of us want to give up the perverse joy of nursing hatred. "I don't want to love that awful person" is a normal reaction.

Unfortunately, many misinterpret forgiveness as allowing a person to continue abusing us. Fortunately, however, true forgiveness does not imply that we become doormats for thoughtless or mean people. On the other hand, today's oppressive, inconsiderate nincompoop could be tomorrow's valued friend. Forgiveness opens that possibility.

A young woman was molested for many years by her father until she reached a point where she wanted to die rather than be subjected to further mistreatment. In desperation she reported her father. Her mother vehemently defended him and was willing to give up her children rather than face the reality of all that was taking place. Even extended family members sided with the parents, calling the child "liar," "bitch," and "whore." Siblings were angry because they, too, were under investigation. The girl found herself alone, feeling guilty and dirty. She had every reason to be bitter.

Her recovery was long and complicated. Abhorrence for her father and her family grew so intense that she found herself caught up in the sordid circumstances. Family hatred became mutually intense when her father was indicted and placed on the docket for trial.

Then it happened! She realized she could forgive her father and the family, but she could never live with them again. She could love them even though they did not reciprocate her love. Loving her father was possible although her testimony would no doubt put him in prison. She need not let hate motivate her. She was determined to rebuild her life and love those who did not want or appreciate her love. Above all, she came to love herself and rejected the attempts of others to make her feel guilty. She refused to let hate ferment. As a result, she grew into a gracious young woman who now has a husband and several children.

One of the most difficult steps toward emotional maturity is learning to love the unlovable. Christian belief stresses God's love for everyone. This is an esoteric ideal, but some of us manage to get better by letting go of hate. At least it promises more fertile soil for love to grow.

Divorced persons often fear that forgiveness means reconciliation and, subsequently, more hurt. Hostility, on the other hand, provides a protective barrier.

Divorce has a purpose, albeit a tragic one. It is a recognized process that officially marks the end of a marital relationship and the hostilities that created emotional disaster. Yet, for many, divorce often does not work any better than marriage; true, the marriage is dissolved but the bitterness remains.

Children caught in the middle of post-divorce warring inevitably suffer. They get expert lessons on holding grudges and retaliation. They may even get coaching to hate the other parent. With minimal effort, the inability to forgive is successfully cloned in the next generation. The only good coming out of this is a new set of clients for tomorrow's marriage counselors.

A technique which has helped many post-divorce parents begin to overcome animosity is actually a simple matter of reframing the relationship into a business relationship rather than a marital one. After all, the purpose of post-divorce communication is primarily business. Insurance policies, medical expenses, school fees, clothing costs, and college funds are just a few of the business items which require ongoing transactions.

Post-divorce forgiveness enables one to discuss business without reinfecting old hurts and disappointments. The "ex" may be unable to do this. But we are only responsible for our own emotional health; we cannot force anyone else to change.

I often suggest that the "ex" be thought of as a banker. We need not love our banker to do business with him. In fact, we may become quite angry if we cannot secure a loan or disagree about interest rates and repayment schedules. Yet, we maintain emotional composure and use our best business skills and decorum.

Perhaps the idea seems too simple but I've asked many post-divorce parents to put a sign on their telephones stating "He (or she) is my banker." This does not assure forgiveness, but it does reduce hostility. After all, we have to start somewhere.

COMMON MENTAL AND EMOTIONAL ROADBLOCKS
"No way, Jose!"

Fear of internal rage

Fear of the intensity of our own anger frequently reinforces resistance. Though we may act civilized, deep inside there can be raging emotional volcanos. This is dangerous because "good" people do not explode or even allow themselves to get teed off.

Several years ago a sixteen-year-old boy was referred to me with a long history of fighting, poor school performance, and threatening adults. Authorities had removed the young man from his home several years prior to the referral. He had lived with relatives, in foster homes, or anywhere else he could hang his hat. As his behavior worsened, he was running out of places to live. A lock-down facility was under consideration.

Mr. Sixteen-year-old was an interesting young man. Our therapy sessions seemed to go well; he became increasingly verbal and was far more articulate than I had expected. As he became more trusting, we developed a healthy rapport. Slowly, he began uncovering deep-seated hurts and frustration. As a little boy, he had spent hours looking through a keyhole watching his mother have sexual relations with one man after another. Eventually, when he was eight or nine years old, she caught him peeping. Her reaction was to take him into the bedroom where she taught him intercourse and oral sex. Later, she abandoned him to an abusive alcoholic stepfather who severely beat him. Emergency room attendants contacted authorities.

The psychotherapy was going well and many unresolved emotional issues were emerging. We were in the middle of a psychotherapeutic gold mine and had struck the main load. But we faced another problem; his behavior was getting worse. Psychotherapy was not working and the psychotherapist was not helping.

During a particularly intense session, I questioned him about his anger toward his mother and planned to ask about dad later. In a convincing tone, he denied having any anger toward her at all. In fact, he believed his life would be better if he could return home and live with her.

Rather than attempt to batter down his obvious resistance, I suggested that he write a letter to his mother and tell her his true feelings. He was not to send it to her but was to bring it to our next session.

A week passed. I really didn't expect him to follow through on my suggestion. After all, he didn't do his homework for school so why should he complete an assignment for me. I was wrong. He brought me the letter. With his permission I share it with you, crude as it is.

Dear Mamma,

You are a low down disgraceful person to the human race. You are a bitch, a slut, a hore, a three time prostitute, and you are a hag. If I were to see you I would tell you to fuck off and go to hell if you were to say I love you, cause if you loved me, you would have taken or come and got me when you left. Well that is all I have to say you damn low down prostitute bitch.

Bye!!!

You are a hag and a slut.
Fuck off Bitch!!!
2 times bitch

The letter is crude—but sacred. It reflects the anger buried deep in the soul of this unfortunate boy. It represents his deepest fear that a raging volcano of hate had replaced love.

Eventually, he harnessed the volcano. He found he could still love someone—someone who had cruelly abused and rejected him. I admired his valiant emotional courage and began to respect his unusual ability to forgive. We both got better.

Fear of sharing too much

Most of us fear to excavate hidden artifacts uncovered by emotional archaeology or confront honestly the internal volcanos of rage. This fear, however, is mild when it is compared with sharing those feelings with someone else. If we cannot trust ourselves with these outcasts of the soul, who can we trust.

Perhaps I can learn to accept myself with these hidden malignancies, but would anyone else love and respect me if they knew of the corruption that infected the very core of my personality? Can I ever face reality again? Will I be catapulted into loneliness? Is it possible for someone to understand and love me in spite of my hatred for those who made me suffer?

Maybe someone, while not necessarily agreeing, will understand and hold our feelings in trust. Healing often begins when we finally open ourselves to another person. Such sharing can be alarming since we become vulnerable and risk more hurt in honest self-disclosure. Choosing the right confidant is crucial and trust is essential.

I have worked with many women who have carried into their adult life the weight of having been sexually molested as children. They are shackled with this dreaded secret and the hatred it generates. They rationalize that keeping it hidden may make it go away and perhaps, in time, may even no longer be true.

Repeatedly, victimized women say, "I've never told anyone about it; it was so long ago. Sometimes, I even convince myself that I had gotten over it only to have it haunt me again." Others say, "I get so depressed and I can't tell my husband. He loves me, but he would never understand." Still others say, "I have never been able to talk about it. Somehow it seems it was my fault and I feel like a whore."

As a therapist, I am humbled with such sacrosanct disclosures. But the most rewarding experience is to witness the forgiveness of these brave women who, with time, resolve their bitterness.

Occasionally, disclosure is insurmountable and forgiveness is more difficult. Nevertheless, the door to the reparative power of therapeutic forgiveness is not necessarily closed. In such instances, it becomes imperative to assess the cost of revealing the depth of the hurt in light of the help one receives.

A word of warning. Therapeutic forgiveness is lost if, by laying bare our hatred for another person, it evolves into a subtle form of revenge. Self-disclosure can be an opportunity to assassinate the character or reputation of the offender. As a therapist, I am not interested in who has caused the damage; I am interested only in healing the malignancy that damage has caused. Who caused it may be a matter for the police, but it has no place in therapeutic disclosure.

Forgiveness is a personal, internal experience that takes place inside the victimized individual. There are no prerequisites from any other person—especially the perpetrator. Forgiveness may be a private experience and no one need ever know whom you have forgiven—or why. However, others may witness beautiful changes in your life and you will find peace.

Fear of emotional expenditure

The fear of emotional expenditure is legitimate. Reognizing the need to forgive requires considerable effort. Sorting out emotional garbage is taxing. Hauling it away is exhausting.

Anger, hate, and hostility are powerful forces. Without them we may feel empty and listless. They are hidden dynamos of destruction that energize our lives. Such insidious drives for retaliation become precious and to give them up seems unthinkable. Living without them could threaten to erase our identities.

I recall a man who was so steeped in alienation toward his ex-wife that he became fixated on his own loathing. These feelings were understandable since she refused to let him see his children despite liberal visiting rights. He was particularly upset to discover she had told the children he despised them and that his feelings were the reason for their divorce. Frustrated, he could not defend himself and assure the children of his love; he was losing them. Hate is a mild word for the intensity of contempt he held for her. Meaning for life evaporated and the loathing became an obsession. He believed he would forfeit everything if he abandoned his loathing.

Forgiveness was like walking through hell, but with guidance from a caring therapist he realized that only forgiveness would extinguish his agony. Giving up his impelling need to "get even" left him temporarily lethargic and depressed. He missed the energy that bitterness generated and he felt psychologically impoverished. But gradually his life was restored. Forgiveness generated newfound internal resources, freeing him from his hatred. Slowly, he won the respect of his children. They continued to love their mother, but they felt she had deceived them by her misrepresentation of their father.

The cost of forgiving becomes more poignant with the realization one must accept the consequences of another's unjust behavior. We may suffer immeasurable pain because someone has wreaked havoc in our lives—in our souls. Often we cannot repair the damage even if the perpetrator chooses to do so. Commonly, offenders do not give a damn about us, much less care how we feel. They may not be remotely interested in repairing the injury, no matter how much we suffer.

To forgive an offense requires that we pay the price of accepting internal distress for another's behavior. We must assume undeserved hurt and give up hope for retaliation. Yes, it is unfair, but unfairness is a part of life. After all, if it were fair we would have no need to forgive.

Fear of forgetting

"I'll forgive but I will never forget" is a nice way of saying, "I will not forgive." Realistically, the ability to forget is an illusive quality. So we may find ourselves caught between our desire to forgive and our inability to forget having been victimized.

Since most of us are not saints, we find ourselves unwilling to forget. Much of the time we even resist forgiving, but to forget on top of forgiving is the final straw. So we may be tempted to ignore forgiveness.

Memory, the very soul of hostility, keeps anger alive. When we blank out memory, we give up a portion of life consciousness that is essential to identity. To forget is to lose a part of self. This is frightening.

Most of us don't want to forget because we perceive the process to be an emotional lobotomy. We recognize the need to forgive but not at the expense of valuable brain centers. After all, significant memory loss is usually a sign of brain disease or damage. Who needs a crushing blow to the head or self-imposed Alzheimer's disease?

I admire people who claim they can forgive and forget. These individuals gladly recite a menu of injuries they have forgotten.

"Selective amnesia" is a feat of mental gymnastics beyond the skill of the average person. Suppression (conscious refusal to think about it) and repression (unconscious refusal) are attempts to accomplish this psychologic double back flip. At times these exercises work reasonably well. But unresolved resentment tends to seep back into the conscious flow of thought or unconsciously becomes displaced on some other undeserving person, thus creating a second generation of suffering.

Some philosophers and theorists suggest the human mind is like a "tablet of wax" (tabula rasa) that ancient scribes used as we use writing paper. In place of the ballpoint pen, scribes used a sharpened stick to make impressions in wax that they poured evenly over a wooden tablet. At birth, an infant's mind is often compared with a smooth fresh tablet where every experience in life is recorded.

A world without paper is hard to imagine. Modern bureaucratic machinery would grind to a halt. But for centuries scribes wrote on anything available. Shards (fragments of broken clay bottles) must have been fun to write on. Wax tablets had a decided advantage; they could be heated or scraped smooth (erased) and used again.

But the human mind is not a tablet of wax. To be sure, memory is a constant ongoing recording process, but the similarities end there. The mind is not so easily erased.

I illustrated this point at a workshop for a sophisticated, informed group of professional people. Stepping to the chalkboard, I wrote the word "shit" in large block letters. I always wanted to do this in the fifth grade, but I was afraid of getting into trouble. Now I was getting paid for it. Needless to say, I offended the group.

I intensified the situation, pointing out that my behavior was premeditated and deliberate and I would not apologize. My audience was now in the crux of decision. Each person had to decide: be outraged and leave the workshop, attempt to control their reactions to my behavior and stay even though they were upset, or forgive me and feel better. To their credit, they forgave me.

We were ready for the next step. I went back to the board, erased the word, and challenged them to forget what I had written. I suggested that if I met anyone in the room a year later they might or might not remember my lectures, but they would remember the word I had written on the board. Eventually, this proved true. These gracious people invited me back and I tested their memory. They had forgiven me, but their memory circuits were still intact.

Neurologists tell us that memories and feelings may indeed be programmed in neural circuits. For instance, Wilder Penfield has conducted some fascinating experiments. He found that stimulating specific points on the exposed brain of conscious subjects caused them to relive past memories and feelings. He was even able to map the location of the circuits.[2] Our past seems to be permanently recorded and cannot be erased without destroying brain tissue. A major roadblock to forgiveness is this physically impossible task of forgetting. Indeed it is impossible if we assume that forgiveness and forgetting are Siamese twins, each mutually dependent on the other.

Forgetting is an attempt to disarm the emotional intensity of justifiable anger, to terminate all hope or need to retaliate or exact compensation. To disarm the potency of hostility is an essential part of forgiveness. Disarming is possible; forgetting is not. To clear this roadblock, we direct our energy toward disarming rather than denying the natural process of memory circuits. Memory does not refire hatred unless we allow it to do so.

To disarm outrage requires a few basic internal commitments. Every individual has personal ownership of each memory. We also have personal responsibility for what we do with those memories. To disarm effectively, we must make a firm decision to bury our hatred; refuse to resurrect it; determine never to use it against the offender; forfeit the desire for vengeance; and finally, continue living and growing as if we had never been injured.

THE PAIN OF VICTIMIZATION
"I'll never rest till justice is done."

Where is justice?

Justice is often an illusive hope and a fickle lady. To base mental, emotional, and spiritual health on our belief that fairness will always win out is folly. Many of us grew up under the influence of Hopalong Cassidy, Superman, and Howdy Doody. We expect the bad guys always to lose and the good ones always to win.

There exists a belief among many today that good and evil must balance. The yin and yang must be equal. The old idiom, "What goes around comes around," expresses the same idea. Somehow we have the notion that someone must pay for every evil act. When we are victimized, we want justice. Often we do not want to forgive, for that would call on us to relinquish our hope of getting even. Ironically, we often lose interest in justice when we are the perpetrator.

I believe every child has the right to a normal home—whatever a normal home is. Every child has the right to a mom, a dad, basic physical essentials, and an emotional environment conducive to healthy development.

Many children who have shared their suffering with me will never experience an equal portion of right and wrong. Irresponsible selfish adults, tragic circumstances, or a combination of both have robbed and cheated an alarming number of them.

A thirteen-year-old friend shared with me an account of unimaginable abuse and tragedy. Her father murdered her mother. Soon thereafter he died from wounds inflicted in a brawl. She also lost a younger sister who died from an incurable disease. Within two months, she lost her maternal grandparents, her only hope for a stable life. One foster home followed another—many were abusive. Shelters, detention halls, and group homes came in succession. In her short life, she had experienced more heartache than most octogenarians ever accumulate.

Through it all, she was able to forgive and was an exemplary genial young woman. She had learned to control her life when all else was out of control. She was one of the first to teach me about the meaning of forgiveness.

To withhold forgiveness until a wrong is made right risks the possibility that we will condemn ourselves to a life sentence of unresolved bitterness. There is no guarantee on fairness and justice, and we cannot always right some wrongs. For instance, I cannot repair the damage of destroying your reputation. Your only hope is to forgive me and heal yourself.

Victims are seldom in a position to demand retribution. I once lost a court case over property damage. The judge's incredulous decision stunned my attorney and me. I had looked to the judicial system— the American way—for justice but found none. Appeal is part of the system, too, but for me it was much too costly and time consuming to be worthwhile. I had to absorb the losses. I had a choice: to forgive or become bitter.

Hope for vengeance

When repayment is not possible, the natural reaction is to seek revenge. Vengeance seems so sweet, so satisfying. I remember the exhilarating feeling I had when I saw a man who betrayed my friendship mash his fingers in a car door. Later, that same feeling turned to shame as I began to deal with the bitterness I had built up. There simply is no therapeutic value in revenge.

After losing his job, an embittered high school teacher commented, "I was raised on the old saying, 'one who takes revenge in less than twenty years acts in haste.' " He went on: "I'm sure twenty years will be enough time to make them wish they had never screwed me over!"

Anger, hurt, and hatred fuel the desire for revenge. It creates a perverted quest for justice. Therapeutic forgiveness transcends vengeance.

Crushed self-esteem

The hope for justice is closely associated with the sense of self-esteem. When we are victimized, we feel powerless, violated, and angry. If we had more power, more resources, more intelligence, we could set the record straight. If we are attacked, we feel worthless and frustrated. Victimization is an assault on our personal dignity. Yet, in reality, it does not erode our person. Victimization does not affect personal worth. But until this is understood, the idea of giving up revenge is unthinkable.

Victims of rape and molestation have taught me a great deal about therapeutic forgiveness. Sexual violation is forgivable, but it is one of the most difficult offenses to resolve. Unfortunately, some programs designed to rehabilitate victims of sexual assault only foster more anger, suspicion, and withdrawal. This is particularly disastrous for victimized women who, understandably, feel hatred toward a perpetrator but who end up hating all men. The end result is another assault on her femininity. Her capacity for healthy love may be devastated. She may be unable to respond intimately with someone she truly loves. Her body heals; her self-esteem remains broken.

Girls who have been sexually victimized over a period of time may turn to sexual promiscuity or become sexually dysfunctional. Having lost their self-esteem, they allow themselves to be used instead of loved. Others associate sexual intimacy with a feeling of degradation which often restricts orgasmic expression. Forgiveness, a major step toward recovering self-esteem, builds character and strength and instills a sense of personal worth.

Forgiveness, however, does not mean one continues to be victimized. Nor does it mean victims cannot take legal or definitive action to prevent criminals and abusers from continuing to wreak havoc on others. We can, indeed, forgive and resolve bitterness but still take whatever steps necessary to execute justice. However, motivation need not be rooted in anger or hope of vengeance. That is poison.

Ongoing resentment only intensifies the damage of victimization.

We subject ourselves to double jeopardy. Victimized once by an offender, we are victimized again by our own hatred. The second victimization usually results in loss of friends, peace of mind, and even serious physical disorders. We are made helpless by the first victimizing, but we can control the second. Forgiveness rebuilds self-esteem; this enables us to recover from victimization.

Victims' rights

Victims' rights is a healthy movement. Far too long criminals have violated the basic rights of others, leaving their victims without recourse. What happens to those who are permanently injured or brain damaged after robberies and muggings? Who pays for the therapy the victims of rape need, especially when they would rather die than resolve their feelings of degradation?

Victimization is particularly frustrating because the victims feel the criminal behavior of others ruthlessly controls them. "An eye for an eye" may seem a satisfactory solution, but the price for personal retribution is loss of control. We become enslaved to our own bitterness. Although it seems improbable, forgiveness is the only antidote to bitterness. We gain control of our innermost selves and we get better.

Families of murder victims often attend the execution of the killer. They feel they cannot reorganize their lives until the criminal is put to death. Some insist they have the right to watch the condemned person die. Perhaps these feelings are understandable, but non-forgiveness may become an incurable emotional malignancy before justice is carried out. To watch another die cannot cure that deep ache in the soul. Capital punishment is indeed punishment, but it will not restore the rights of victims or rehabilitate the criminal. There is no healing; it is just another tragic death.

Must forgiveness be paid for in blood? Some people believe so and cite biblical precedents to support their position. Human selfishness and hatred may result in bloodshed, but is that the price of forgiveness or is it the consequence of violent behavior?

Forgiveness is not something we do for another; rather, we do it for ourselves, for peace of mind, and for growth. Perpetrators may or may not know of the forgiveness; it is the exclusive domain of the victims.

Victims are entitled to rage, frustration, and bitterness. Without the right to seethe in anger, we would have no need to forgive. But as victims we also have the right to forgive.

Recognizing the Need to Forgive

Automobile maintenance is one of my weekend diversions. On one such day, I noticed the brake pedal was not working properly and the problem wasn't getting any better. I finally had to admit that further driving was dangerous. I parked the car, not knowing what was wrong. Intelligence is not necessarily what we know, but our ability to find out. Upon checking the brakes, an experienced mechanic diagnosed the problem as worn brake pads. I now knew what to do. I replaced the pads and the brakes were fully restored.

My point is that I had to recognize the need for new brakes. Until then, I was a danger to myself and to everyone on the streets. Apply this analogy to the need to forgive. Forgiveness has no meaning, relevance, or application until it becomes a personal need. Ingrained bitterness rarely cures itself and can become increasingly dangerous.

One major reason we overlook forgiveness as a cure for personal bitterness is the inability to recognize a need for it. Hostility may be disguised so well that it is not seen as an emotional disorder. Bitterness can creep slowly into our lives until, eventually, it becomes an integral part of our personalities. Unwittingly we host parasites of emotional disease that exist as long as they live in us.

Recognizing the need to forgive does not come easily or naturally. Anger, hostility, vengeance, and hate are normal but destructive; they upset the balance of emotional homeostasis and lead to terminal bitterness. Forgiveness as a means of therapeutic intervention is not a normal process. Paradoxically, we learn to do something abnormal to overcome a natural process so we can become normal again.

Understanding the need to forgive may be as confronting as a need for plastic surgery. Maxwell Maltz offers some fascinating insights into therapeutic forgiveness in his book, *Psycho-cybernetics*. His perspective as a plastic surgeon is interesting. These few quotations may be meaningful:

FORGIVENESS IS A SCALPEL
WHICH REMOVES EMOTIONAL SCARS

Therapeutic forgiveness cuts out, eradicates, cancels, makes the wrong as if it had never been. Therapeutic forgiveness is like surgery .... In removing old emotional scars, you alone can do the operation. You must become your own plastic surgeon—and give yourself a spiritual face-lift. The results will be new life and new vitality, a new-found peace of mind and happiness.

To speak of an emotional face-lift and the use of "mental surgery" is more than a simile.

Old emotional scars cannot be doctored or medicated. They must be "cut out," given up entirely, eradicated....

I can only tell you as a doctor that if you will do it you will be far happier, healthier, and attain more peace of mind. However, I would like to point out that this is what therapeutic forgiveness is, and that it is the only type of forgiveness that really works. And if forgiveness is anything less than this, we might as well stop talking about it ....

You'll actually look younger. Many times I have seen a man or a woman apparently grow five or ten years younger in appearance after removing old emotional scars.[1]

Identifying our emotional garbage is a prerequisite for recognizing the need to forgive. In their book, *Guide to Recovery: A Book for Adult Children of Alcoholics,* Herbert Gravitz and Julie Bowden cite an old proverb: "The beginning of wisdom is to call things by their right name."[2] How true! There can be no substitute for absolute self-honesty. Those who learn to forgive are brave and strong people who courageously call their own bitterness by its right name and venture to conquer it.

Early lessons on reality distortion
"Why should I forgive; it was my fault."

All parents make mistakes

Because I am a family therapist, parents often drag their children to me expecting an instant fix for the child who will not mind or rebels against the chaos at home. Problems may include poor grades, back talk, sibling rivalry, refusal to do chores, fidgeting, or other conflicts found in all homes. The child is cited as the "identified patient" who has a problem. Parents complain, "I've tried everything!" As these children grow up, they assume guilt for the whole family. Forgiving themselves becomes a serious issue.

The problem is not necessarily the child; it is the parents. Some parents find it unthinkable to admit their need for help. They reshape reality and make the child responsible for the family's misery. By distorting reality, adults can more easily admit having a problem child and ask for help at the same time. Some families even see therapy for their "disturbed child" as a status symbol.

After a few sessions with the child, I schedule parent conferences when the child is not with them. When Mom and Dad get better, the child gets better via remote control. The most difficult children are those whose parents are not accessible; for example, those living in institutional homes.

There are really no normal homes, but some are more conducive to emotional maturity than others. Parents may vehemently deny family conflict, yet I get a different picture from a child when I ask, "Who is the champion screamer in your home?" Parents usually get somewhat solemn, but a more accurate picture of reality emerges. Children love this.

In other cases, parents subtly warn children against disclosing family dysfunction. It is not unusual for parents to answer simple questions for their children or to see youngsters take their cues from their parents or get permission to answer the questions. Family therapists are familiar with these unspoken conspiracies. In extreme cases, children are not allowed to test reality. They do not realize they are the scapegoat for deeper family problems. They do not perceive a need to forgive because they have never had to clarify this form of mental abuse.

Parents have unimaginable influence over the development of their children. Most of us panic when we see our problems emerging in them. This is especially true when we are unrealistic with ourselves. We can do a lot of damage but we can also prevent much misery. The irony in this is that about the time we become grandparents we may have finally learned to parent.

Most parents love their children. This includes abusive parents. In spite of their lack of impulse control, poor personal judgment, emotional immaturity, and selfishness, their children experience both love and abuse. Such a contrast of mixed messages prods these youngsters to search desperately for reality.

Gravit and Bowden present a valuable description of chemically dependent dysfunctional families. Their perception is valid for all ailing families, regardless of cause. Citing Claudia Black's well-known rules found in homes with alcoholic parents, "Don't talk, don't trust, don't feel," they point out that children cannot adequately grasp reality under these circumstances.[3]

The mother of one little girl who had been placed in a children's home told the child, "If you ever want to come home, watch what you say to that nosey social worker. She has it in for Bill (the mother's live-in boyfriend) since you lied about what he did to you. How could you have done this to me!" A year in therapy did not resolve the child's confusion.

Talking, trusting, and feeling are viewed as exclusive rights of adults. Children in families where there is strong pathologic enmeshment find themselves as serfs in a family fiefdom the parents have structured for their own convenience. These parental warlords rule their feudal estates with an iron hand but don't fulfill their adult responsibilities. Many of these unfortunate children, functioning as miniature adults, do not have the "rights and privileges thereunto appertaining."

For many youngsters who grow up in these circumstances, forgiveness is irrelevant. They see nothing to forgive and cannot imagine life any other way. They grow up, choose dysfunctional mates, and clone themselves—misery and all. Perpetually unhappy in their innate anger and hostility, they simply do not recognize it nor do they know how to live without it.

These children feel worthless and blame themselves. They experience a deprivation to speak, trust, or have feelings—feelings that are important to others. For them to trust someone enough to talk about their feelings is unthinkable. These children are so internally angry that their parents fear adequate and appropriate expression from them. Expressing anger and hostility is too dangerous and the consequences are too grave emotionally and physically. These youngsters find it easier to deny their anger or hostility because it is safer to assume blame and remain passive. Many wait for the opportune time to lash out at someone less threatening than an abusive, unpredictable parent. Unfortunately, the opportune time usually comes when they are older and stronger, and someone gets hurt.

A five-year-old girl was so enmeshed with her warring parents that her perception of real or unreal was seriously warped. Both parents chided, coached, and emotionally coerced her to accuse the other of sexual abuse. Soon she was giving accounts that were not possible. Most professionals know it is rare for a five year old to fabricate sexual abuse, but this was a case of two selfish, immature parents who lashed out at each other with such vicious intensity that their child lost her grip on reality. Will she ever forgive them?

Precognitive limbo land

Family traditions offer children a sense of security. It is an effort to make sense out of our perception of reality, values, and our place in the schema of the universe.

Growing up with rough and tumble brothers, we had little appreciation for tradition. But one of our family customs is unforgettable. We celebrated birthdays with candles on a cake of our choice. Before we lit the candles, my father would recite the events of the day we were born. He recalled how we looked and why we were special. This became meaningful and offered a glimpse into our precognitive lives.

Children love to hear about themselves and learn about their infancy. During clinical interviews, children are usually spellbound when parents talk about their child's early developmental accomplishments. They love to hear about their learning to crawl, walk, talk, and when their first tooth appeared.

Adults, not children, resist coming to grips with precognitive or early childhood issues. Many adults become angry in therapy when facts and early memories of hurt, rejection, and abuse surface. If one is unable to forgive, these experiences and memories are apt to be unbearable.

Sigmund Freud sparked intense interest in early childhood development. Elaborating on his observation of the oral, anal, and genital stages, he theorized that neurotic or hysterical behavior has its roots in these phases of life. Consequently, several generations blame their problems on inept parents, mysterious libidinal forces, or faulty potty training.

A word of caution. An archaeological trip into our own precognitive limbo may yield insights into quirks in our personalities.

However, this does not imply that we cannot change who we are, what we are, what we are doing, or where we are going. We will always be responsible for ourselves. True, we did not choose our parents nor did we control how they treated us. Yet, we cannot claim our right to human autonomy unless we assume responsibility for shaping or reshaping our own lives. Forgiving our parents makes this possible, and we pray our children will do the same.

Developmental psychologists tell us that considerable programming takes place early in our existence. Important developmental milestones such as bonding—that special comforting love usually between mother and child—and trust occur long before memory, self-awareness, and the ability to reason. Of course, love and trust radically affect our ability to forgive.

During these early stages of life, children learn specific coping skills. Precognitive attempts to solve problems shape our personality.

Gravitz and Bowden refer to this phenomenon as "survival," which may be the most important of all developmental tasks. The more chaotic the environment, the more sophisticated the survival techniques become. They assert that children develop their own rules to enable them to live in the midst of emotional havoc:

- "If I don't talk, nobody will know how I feel, and I won't get hurt.
- "If I don't ask, I can't get rejected.
- "If I'm invisible, I'll be okay.
- "If I'm careful, no one will get upset.
- "If I stop feeling, I won't have any pain.
- "I must make things as safe as possible."[4]

These survival rules are particularly relevant to recognizing the need to forgive. To acknowledge that need is to break each rule. To forgive may seem to threaten our survival when, actually, we have assured it.

Emotional astigmatism

Astigmatism is a condition of the eyes that causes imperfect images or distorted vision. It is a description of common emotional misperception as well.

People probably use denial more than any other form of emotional warping. When one gets a false, unclear, or blank emotional printout, forgiveness may have little or no meaning. We must have a clear image of who we need to forgive and why.

Emotional astigmatism is an "art" usually learned early in life. Distorting emotions works quite well in the heat of childhood conflict, but it is not serviceable later in life when circumstances change.

I am reminded of a nine-year-old friend who was having extreme problems adjusting to placement in a group home. A major obstacle was bedwetting, more of a problem to the staff than to him. In time, he shared with me how cruelly his mother had rejected him and put him out of her home to make room for a new boyfriend. His natural father took him for a while, but he had no time for the boy nor interest in him. Eventually, he was turned over to the county.

One day we broached the subject of bedwetting. Wistfully, he recalled how warm his mother's body felt when she once held him. My young friend remembered that she took good care of him—even changing his wet clothes. Before the session was over, it was evident that he was searching for his mother's love, using his own urine as a substitute for her warmth and attention. He got better.

Clinicians must exercise great care with children who survive by twisting their emotions into feelings they find more acceptable and less threatening. Youngsters often create a halo over destructive parents. The more dysfunctional the parent, the brighter the halo tends to be. Many manufacture a "parent ideal" in their efforts to maintain some kind of emotional equilibrium. They perceive their parents as saintly and never in need of forgiveness.

Children also frequently feel intense loyalty to abusive parents, but in serious cases they must be removed from their homes. These youngsters will usually blame the system and will do anything to get back with their parents. Some suffer abuse, molestation, or neglect in silence rather than be disloyal or acknowledge that mom or dad is cruelly sick. Therefore, they never consider the need to forgive.

Many of my young friends placed with agencies have periodic home visits. They view these visits as brief trips to heaven, even when they are neglected, abused, or exposed to cold-blooded savagery. Some have even witnessed beatings, knifings, shootings, and murder, yet they tend to distort what has actually happened. Ironically, many blame themselves.

Protective service workers must terminate harmful visits for the child's safety. When I inquire about these broken visits, I get typical emotional astigmatic answers: "It was fine," "I had a good time," "Mom and Dad were okay." They simply cannot deal with their feelings and it is easier to believe their own misperceptions. Forgiveness is as relevant to them as Latin is to a duck.

Emotional astigmatism allows the child to accept the unacceptable and even prosper in it. Many find they cannot live without chaos. Often, in healthy foster homes they feel like fish out of water. They are unable to talk about feelings—especially their own; they cannot trust and often engineer rejection; they do not feel worthy of love.

As a result, they never become aware of the importance of forgiveness. The world of honest feelings remains in a myopic blur. To admit the need to forgive their parents is an admission of the reality of their parents' brutality. So unresolved anger, frustration, and hostility go unrecognized, fermenting deep inside into adult bitterness.

Adult slopover

Early lessons in reality distortion have long-range effects. Those ingenious rules for survival are carried into adult life. The problem is that what worked in childhood does not work in adult life. Consequently, chronological adults attempt to solve problems like children.

For instance, children naturally express themselves and solve their frustrations by fighting. I can put a couple of three year olds in a playroom with five hundred toys, but within a few minutes they will be fighting over the same toy. Most of us are aware of how vicious three year olds can be. They hit each other over the head and knock each other down; that necessitates soft toys for small children. Combat is unacceptable normal behavior for this age group.

I often point this out to older boys and girls who are still fighting as a means to solve problems. Teenagers develop muscles and physical strength; some learn to use weapons. For them, solving problems like three year olds becomes dangerous. Those who cannot learn more mature problem-solving skills eventually end up abusing spouses and children. Prisons are full of people with adult bodies and three-year-old emotional maturity levels.

The earlier appropriate problem-solving skills are learned, the less traumatic the lesson. This is also true of forgiveness. In my experience, children have more difficulty recognizing the need to forgive, but they find forgiveness easier once they accomplish it. Adults are better at recognizing the need, but they have more difficulty putting forgiveness into practice.

The lack of consistent parental discipline is a common denominator among emotionally disturbed children. Latch-key children are more numerous than ever before. Older siblings may attempt to take on parental responsibility for younger brothers and sisters, but they lack the needed authority or wisdom to be consistent. Consequently, many grow up without the benevolent but firm structure essential for the development of self-discipline.

Adults who have not learned self-discipline can no longer look to parents to fill the deficit. One must learn it for oneself. Likewise, if we do not learn forgiveness in childhood, we must teach it to ourselves. Self-discipline enables us to achieve a more rewarding level of forgiveness and personal maturation.

Teenagers are anxious to become men and women. Fifteen year olds usually think they are twenty while their parents see them as being twelve. It's a confusing but wonderful period of life. Adolescence is a time when young men and women firm their concepts of masculinity and femininity. This is an excellent time to teach emotional maturity. There is more to life than physical strength and the ability to procreate. To grow into real men and women also includes emotional and spiritual growth. People who learn to forgive are men and women who stand as stalwart examples for us all.

As grown-ups, we tend to continue denying, repressing, suppressing, and minimizing our hurts. We use adult freedom to express anger, fury, venom, and malice. With more power, we become increasingly able to inflict our bitterness on ourselves and others. The need to learn and practice forgiveness becomes more urgent. In the final analysis, forgiveness becomes the ultimate survival skill.

SELF-APPRAISAL AND DAMAGE CONTROL
"But I have a right to hate."

Giving up old defenses

Old defenses are like lifelong friends. They have worked so well that we build our personalities around them. Would we have an identity if we were stripped of these shields, or would we feel naked and vulnerable?

Physical nudity does not threaten as much as psychological nudity. We can take clothes off and put them back on, but emotional disclosure is forever. This prompts many to drop out of psychotherapy when defenses start to crumble.

For instance, if I minimize my anger at someone who has outraged my dignity, I will not have to deal with the fact that I loathe his guts. I am a nice person, and it's hard to allow conscious recognition of such feelings. It is easier to say, "It really doesn't matter." That is one way of keeping my nice-guy image. But I risk displacing my feelings onto someone else: aggression, or taking it out on myself: depression.

The truth is, it does matter. I'm a worthwhile human being, but I'm mad as hell. My real feelings dictate that the person is a son-of-a-bitch and life's greatest pleasure would be to stomp his butt. Furthermore, his behavior validates my feelings.

With feelings like this, can I ever forgive? Yes; it is my only hope. It is not healthy to convert these feelings into internalized bitterness or to act them out in an attack on another person. Such feelings may be real, but if left unattended they endanger my emotional health. I have no mature choice but to forgive. I have to get better.

An advantage to being an adult is that it permits us to be honest with our feelings and to take definitive action as long as we do not harm ourselves or others. As a child, I was not allowed to use bad words. My first grade teacher kept a bar of Ivory soap in her desk. I ate most of it before the year was over, but it was safer to use profanity at school than at home. Besides, the other children admired my ability to eat soap. Today I have an appreciation for the contribution of profanity to the English language. A well-chosen "damn" or "hell" can be richly expressive. Overuse of profanity can, of course, indicate excessive hostility and bitterness.

As mature people, we are also free to give up old defenses. We no longer fear parental punishment and are responsible for our own behavior and feelings. Parental approval is welcome but adults can survive without it.

Old defenses may come down slowly, but they will remain in place unless we work diligently to tear them down to make room for growing into more forgiving and compassionate people.

Repressed anger is particularly difficult because it is an unconscious process. We are not lying when we deny having repressed anger. We simply are not aware of it. But repression glosses over the need to forgive.

To bring repressed anger into the conscious mind may take professional help. However, we are often able to help ourselves by replaying traumatic scenes, becoming acquainted with the feelings we experienced at the time we were hurt. Once exhumed, we can forgive repressed angry feelings.

We need not repress anger to obscure our need to forgive. Any defense that causes us to avoid dealing with actual feelings is sufficient. Common defenses include:

- If I deal with my impulses and feelings, no one will love me, my parents will not approve, I will lose my friends.
- Because anger and hostility are such negative and intense feelings there is no way to deal with them in a pleasant way. It would be like lancing an emotional boil.
- If I admit I am angry and hostile, I will have to step down from my position of moral superiority.
- Relinquishing my rage will force me to give up my hope of controlling the offender. After all, anger, threats, and disapproval controlled most of us in childhood.

Forgiveness would be more popular and life less complicated if we didn't have to relinquish our mechanisms for keeping anger sealed over. Forgiving may appear difficult, but keeping inner monsters at bay requires energy. We could use that same energy to build and become happier people.

As parents, we can help our children learn appropriate ways of expressing anger so that they will not need the defenses we have so carefully cultured. When we see anger in our youngsters, most of us are threatened because we know the misery it can cause. We love them and hope they never experience the hostility we find stirring just under the surface of our own emotional caldrons.

Children need to be taught healthy expressions of anger. It is not an exclusive right of adulthood nor will it be eradicated in children by denying them expression—the key is healthy expression. Some teaching guidelines I offer parents include:

- Set an example. Emotional hysteria is usually learned behavior.
- Realize and accept the fact that children get angry. It is normal.
- Establish a cool-down period. You and the children need it.
- Encourage healthy expression. It is okay to be angry; it is not okay to be disrespectful or destructive.

- Be consistent. You may disagree with their feelings but be ready to understand.

Giving up defenses and discovering raw anger or hostility are not pleasant but this can be healthy. Overcoming defenses helps to uncover the need to forgive and begin healing. It can make the difference between bitter and better.

A sharper picture

"Warning: The Surgeon General has determined that cigarette smoking causes cancer." This seems to be a simple clear message, but those who read it interpret it from their own perspective. I love to smoke. For years, I viewed the Surgeon General as a do-gooder, heading a movement of malcontents who did not like the smell of cigarettes (I think tobacco has a wonderful smell). However, postmortem comparisons of the lungs of smokers with nonsmokers forced me to reevaluate my interpretation. I had to admit my addiction to nicotine and begin a process of recovery now in its fifth year. The point is, we hear what we want to hear. If reality is not clear, we can usually justify our behavior and refuse to change it.

As a psychotherapist, I occasionally hear myself quoted—more often misquoted—as making bizarre recommendations. Ethics of confidentiality don't allow me to do little more than be amused at these mutations of what I actually said. These distortions are not lies nor intentional misrepresentations. They simply bear out the fact that we hear what we want to hear.

Other twisted messages include such statements as "My doctor told me a little whiskey was good for my heart" (translated to as much as a fifth a day). "My therapist told me I would have a nervous breakdown if I didn't leave her." "The cardiologist said I would have a heart attack if I didn't get more help around the house." These are also good examples of the emotional astigmatism we discussed earlier.

A sharper picture is important, but the task of sharpening the picture is different for every individual. Each of us has our internal unique issues to clarify. We need to adjust the lens to bring our struggles into focus. We may help one another, but we must sharpen the image of our personal feelings and accept clear responsibility for our own needs to forgive.

Inside, each of us may be angry—at different people for different reasons—at different levels of intensity. But we have in common a need to forgive and to incorporate therapeutic forgiveness into our lives. We did not grow up in the same homes, marry the same spouse, work for the same people, or have the same friends, yet we all have been subject to deep hurts, many of them barbarous, cruel, and intentional. The challenge is to sharpen the picture until we become aware of whom and why we need to forgive.

One particular mask we use to disguise anger deserves special consideration. Passive-aggression is particularly insidious. It is seldom recognized in the affected person or correctly identified by those who are barbed by it. The need to forgive is varnished over. Passive-aggression is a backwards way of expressing anger. Procrastination, forgetting, slow downs, doing a job but doing it poorly, sulking, and verbal silence are ways of expressing anger in nonaggressive yet irritating ways. Passive-aggressive behaviors range all the way from stubbornness in children to full-blown personality disorders in adults.

Passive-aggressive people may view themselves as saintly; actually, they are heavily vested in subtle revenge. They see no need to forgive others and others wonder why these people are so irksome. The passive-aggressive person hides anger under indifference and may appear pious, innocent, and victimized. In reality, passive-aggression is a means of expressing anger and hostility. When identified correctly, it is belligerent, retaliatory behavior and an indicator that a forgiving attitude is in short supply.

Sometimes sharpening the picture is relatively easy. The offense and damage are obvious. For instance, I had some treasured antiques stolen in a robbery. I didn't have to sharpen the picture to recognize my anger. It isn't likely that we'll ever get the thief or recover the treasures. I was absorbed with the monetary and aesthetic loss and angry with myself for not having had the items insured. In this experience, my feelings were clear enough to move ahead with getting better. I should be so fortunate with other issues.

An absolute commitment to self-honesty is vital to a sharper picture. We need not blame others for our misbehavior nor do we need to assume blame for the behavior of others. Recognizing that others—especially significant others—have hurt us may be emotionally threatening, but it is a more honest way of dealing with our true feelings.

A sharper picture enables us to recognize our fear of internal rage, drive for revenge, and commitment to hate. We can begin to design a new picture with a view toward becoming better, more forgiving people.

Assess the mess

Failure to forgive can cause as much—even more—damage than the original offense. Assessment can reinforce our right to hate and retaliate. But without the damage there is no need to forgive. The fact that we have been hurt, abused, wronged, or damaged is validation for the need to forgive.

When we assess the mess it becomes clear that our emotions— perhaps our lives—have been laid waste by the malicious behavior of someone else. In effect, we may have allowed that person's behavior to control our mental health. But the real mess is within ourselves. The mess is what is happening in us, not what someone else has done to us. Without serious intervention, the mess gets worse and bitterness is born.

To take inventory of damage may not be as frightening as it seems. Keep in mind that taking inventory does not make the problem worse. This is especially helpful when we assess damage someone we love has caused. To be angry and recognize our hurt does not mean we must stop loving. On the other hand, loving someone does not mean we must allow them to control our feelings or subject ourselves to their abuse. It is okay to be angry at someone we love; real love will survive. It is also permissible to put a premium on our own worth as a person and take steps to insure protection from the aberrant behavior of those who couldn't care less about our welfare.

Theodore Rubin in *The Angry book* made an important distinction between "anger" and "slush." Anger is essentially our reaction to specific frustrating events; slush is the internalization of numerous angers which become so entangled with each other that they become indistinguishable.[5]

Taking a cue from Rubin, I have helped many children assess internal damage. To be hurt by those who should love them is particularly confusing. We begin by talking about eating all the chocolate candy we could possibly hold. Pretending to have eaten the very last piece, we imagine one of the pieces has a worm in it. We make believe the worm makes us sick. Angry children tend to delight in vivid grossness so we talk about "a big puke." The word vomit or regurgitate somehow doesn't capture the imagination of angry children. Stirring through the puke, we try to identify which piece of candy made us sick. We label each chocolate with a hurtful event and sometimes draw graphic pictures of separate "globs of puke." We may even find the half-digested worm. Identifying the problem(s) is a monumental step toward forgiveness. This internal examination of bitterness works equally well for adults.

Appraising damage within ourselves is very personal. The World War II military term SNAFU (Situation Normal All Fouled Up) expresses the frustration most of us feel. Hope for rebuilding may seem remote.

Natural and man-made calamity is a tragic part of life. Wars, accidents, violent crimes, fires, floods, tornadoes, and hurricanes take heavy tolls. In shock, survivors try to reason why and wonder if life can continue. Agony is particularly excruciating when loved ones are lost. Yet, devastation cannot overcome the human struggle for survival. A renewed strength emerges with a determination to rebuild and there arises compassion for other victims. Disaster victims cannot get better or rebuild as long as they are bogged down in despair. A vision of getting better and rebuilding is essential.

What is true for disaster victims is equally true when we are faced with forgiving someone who has left our lives in ruins. Refusing to forgive only adds to the destruction, leaving our lives looking more like a war zone than the happy person we would like to be.

Unassessed damage feeds emotional havoc. Unresolved anger toward parents can ruin a marriage. Glossed over hostility can cause depression. Self-pity and a caustic attitude drive friends away. Preoccupation with wounds creates self-centeredness and love turns to hate. Physical problems may grow in the fertile soil of emotional spoilage. A host of cardiovascular and gastrointestinal disorders associated with stress easily takes root.

Fortunately, assessing emotional wreckage can bring about a renewed human spirit. There is always hope for rebuilding, and forgiven bitterness can be bulldozed and buried. A new and better life is built atop the debris. Life is what you make it.

Repair estimate

Rebuilding in a flood-prone area may be chancy. Building planners speculate on the chances of having new construction destroyed by hurricanes, tornadoes, or other acts of God. Insurance companies calculate risks with computers. But options may be more limited when it comes to reconstructing lives. We have only one life and cannot rebuild to become someone else. We can only reconstruct our own lives.

Whether we are estimating the cost of reconstructing real estate or our emotional lives, it is wise to plan ahead. Martin Luther King proclaimed, "I have a dream." He spoke of freedom at a cost. Repairing emotional devastation can set us free from the self-imposed slavery of hostility and hatred. But like any other freedom, we must consider the price.

Estimating the cost of repair requires a blueprint of vision. It may be hard to imagine life sans bitterness. Some may never have known any other way. It is helpful to find another person, then, who exemplifies a forgiving spirit. No one is perfect, but the world is filled with wonderful people whose lives confirm that the price is worthwhile. They give us hope.

At times we may recapture a vision of better times from the past. Marriage counselors often ask couples to recall their happiness when they were dating. The challenge is to pay the price necessary to regain that happiness. It was possible once; it could be possible again.

The cost of repair means we pay to rebuild what someone else has destroyed.

We must estimate the cost of repair versus the cost of continuing in bitterness. Forgiveness will cost our right to hate. We will have to relinquish priceless ammunition in our arsenal for retaliation. But what is the cost of an "eye for an eye"? If we have lost one eye, is it worth risking the other?

The mess and the cost of repair may appear to be overwhelming. We convince ourselves that we will waste our efforts. One cannot argue this point if the focus is on changing the offender. Attempting to change someone else is usually not cost effective.

Considering cost can be dismaying because it is usually heavy. In the final analysis, however, the cost is nothing less than the long-term investment of ourselves. But betterness pays handsome returns.

Unless we change ourselves, repair is impossible. No one can force us to change nor can we force anyone else. Human beings can and do change. "I cannot change" really means "I will not change."

We are all familiar with these retorts: "I've always been this way," or "I can't help it; hot tempers run in my family." When I hear these excuses, I am reminded that humans change; donkeys don't. Donkeys live today just as they did in the time of Balaam. Refusing to change when we could be better is to make an ass of ourselves.

ASSUMING RESPONSIBILITY
FOR OUR REAL FEELINGS
"Hey, this is hurting me!"

Who owns the mess?

An emotional mess is not threatening until it becomes personal. Gravitz and Bowden cite a proverb that expresses the dilemma of accepting ownership of our negative emotional predicaments: "The truth will make you free, but first it will make you miserable." [6]

In graduate school we were taught the difference between "sympathy" and "empathy." Sympathy is taking on emotionally another person's problems—assuming ownership of feeling for another. Empathy is the ability to understand another person without owning their problems—feeling with another. This skill is a means of emotional survival. An effective therapist must be a feeling and caring person but one who cannot let the load of pain he encounters in everyday clinical practice crush him.

I have never totally separated sympathy and empathy. By doing so, I would lose something in therapeutic relationships. Yet, by ascertaining who owns the problems, I have survived years of intense clinical experience. When forgiveness becomes necessary, I have learned to assume ownership for my own mess, regardless of who caused it. Not only have I survived, but I am also getting better.

Each of us must claim our personal mess and allow others that same privilege. Mutual support and understanding are helpful. But the emotional wreckage of hate and hostility are not hot potatoes to be tossed back and forth.

Animosity and anger are emotions we choose to experience. It is impossible for another person to make us mad. I attempt to help youngsters understand this, pointing out that some people get angry over insults while others become angry on one occasion but not on another. A few seem immune altogether. The simple sociogram on the next page illustrates the point.

Child A sends the same message to Child B and Child C (Figure

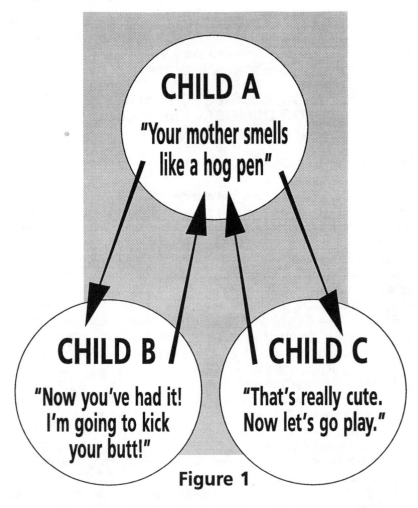

Figure 1

1). Yet B and C respond differently. B chooses to become angry and retaliate while C chooses to respond more maturely and perhaps salvage a friendship.

Choosing how we feel, react, or respond applies also to adults. The emphasis is on choice. We can choose to be "mad" or "unmad"; likewise, we can choose to be "forgiving" or "unforgiving." The choice is ours.

To assume ownership of the mess is to assume responsibility for cleaning it up. We either live in it or we clean it up. Someone else owns the offense. Owning the mess is not pleasant, but it gives the right to rebuild.

Who is hurting?

The answer to this rhetorical question is succinctly expressed in an old spiritual, "It's me, O Lord!" No matter now hurt , angry, or hostile we are, we alone suffer from our damaged feelings. The hope that we can transfer the hurt to perpetrators is the basis for vengeance. It does not work.

Hurting is particularly savage when it is undeserved, when we are at the mercy of someone who takes perverse pleasure in our suffering. Sadistic people relish the power they exert over us. We may lie awake at night seething with anger and pain while they rest comfortably. It is easy to become jealous of their callousness, but such jealousy is a serious symptom of bitterness which only magnifies our pain.

Hurt can stem from personal and impersonal mistreatment. Impersonal victimization is largely a matter of random chance. For instance, when hoodlums snatch a woman's purse, they simply take the first convenient purse. Personal victimization is equally frustrating but hurts more. The following are some examples.

- Personal put-downs to make the other person look better.
- Character assassination which allows heartless people to attire themselves in mock righteousness.
- Personal vilification to express jealousy or revenge.
- Personal gossip to relieve boredom and stimulate sick minds.
- Any offense that is perpetrated on us because of who we are.

The hurt of rejection is one of the most devastating injuries a human can experience. In bereavement, we may feel a loved one has rejected us and abandoned us. Children who suffer emotional or physical rejection are often damaged for life. They learn to withhold trust because they fear they can be hurt again. Some become unable to experience happiness. In the midst of agony, they remain closed up, unable to feel.

To avoid rejection, some couples stay in destructive marital relationships. Beatings or failing to protect children is a price a few willingly pay to escape the agony of rejection by an abusive spouse. Forgiving rejection is not easy; we must first deal with excruciating pain.

Often abusive relationships are cyclic and dependent people feel alone and frightened. Some may break free temporarily only to return for more mental or physical battering. Feelings of desolation are unbearable. Others remain in destructive relationships as their only hope for love. Stuck in reverse, they find it easier to assume guilt for a sick relationship and hope the rejecting abusive partner will forgive them.

Such relationships may end eventually. A few end in murder. However, most broken, self-defeating relationships are repeated with other partners in a series of marriages or live-in arrangements. Many end up alone in mid-life. Suicide attempts are not uncommon. Some never learn to deal with hurt when it happens. Pain does not just go away.

Forgiveness does not imply that we suffer in silence or subject ourselves to further abuse. It does mean the pain is real and becomes our responsibility to heal. Fortunately, forgiveness leads to personal healing and growth; thus, destructive relationships are unnecessary for emotional survival.

Clearly focusing on our hurt may seem to make it worse. However, this is not true. We are merely becoming more responsive and responsible for our innermost needs. We carry out our responsibility for healing only after we accept ownership of our pain.

A word of caution is appropriate. To experience directly the intensity of our hurt may fuel the craving for vengeance. To allow this to happen sabotages the quest for mature responsibility. Emotional immaturity and irresponsibility compound hurt.

The earlier we learn to accept hurt and to forgive, the easier the lesson. Glenn Doman, noted authority on teaching children to read, discovered that even youngsters who had lost significant amounts of brain tissue can be taught to read. He pointed out that early childhood is an amazing period of learning. Brain growth is eighty percent completed at age five and virtually completed at age eight. [7]

Responsibility for dealing with our damaged feelings is also best learned in early childhood. Fortunately, however, it is never too late to learn. But the longer we avoid responsibility for resolving hurt, the more entrenched the bitterness becomes. If children with a partial brain can learn to read, surely we can learn to forgive.

Who can repair the damage?

The answer is clear. We are personally and solely responsible for repairing the damage. Even though someone else caused the wreckage, we cannot repair it unless we do the job ourselves. We may be the only one who really cares. Friends who understand and offer encouragement are treasures and make repair more palatable. They may give bad advice but we can forgive them for that because, usually, they care and want to help. That means a great deal. In the final analysis, though, we must repair our own internal damage.

Forgiveness may be the only tool that really repairs emotional damage. We have seen how immature defenses only gloss over feelings; efforts to change other people fail; an "eye for an eye" repairs nothing. While forgiveness may be the last resort, it should have been our first response.

From time to time, a client asks about reconciliation when a relationship is beyond repair. For instance, post-divorce readjustment can be traumatic for children. They often attempt to get their parents back together. Fortunately, people with irreconcilable differences can forgive each other. Children, too, can forgive their parents. Differences remain but hostility and hatred are eradicated. Forgiveness prevents further damage; healing begins.

Forgiveness does not invite or allow further hurt. Relationships may be beyond repair but individuals who are willing to forgive are always salvageable.

Every now and then the miracle of Humpty Dumpty takes place when a hopeless relationship is cemented back together. This is not the normal course of events, but therapeutic forgiveness is not normal either.

Following emotional devastation, the sooner self-reconstruction begins, the better. Emotional repair takes hard work but once bitterness has set in, the stench of emotional decomposition complicates the task. Rebuilding based on forgiveness anticipates peace and tranquility. A new way of life, a new attitude, a new happiness emerge as new goals. One of my toddler friends said it best, "I feel more better."

Assuming responsibility for repairing damage someone else has done is not as threatening as it might seem. With courage, we can make emotional repairs. In fact, no one can make them for us. Repairs are the exclusive responsibility of every individual.

Parents often put their children in therapy for instant repair. Prior to final tests, parents desperately ask me to overhaul their son or daughter before they fail the school year. Most of these youngsters have been failing all year; some, for the second or third time. Parents hope I have a magic wand which will suddenly transform them into geniuses.

I would so like to perform such magic and meet their expectations. Unfortunately, there are no magic wands. These parents are loving but desperate. Each student must restore his or her own performance level. I can help to motivate, but I cannot do it for them; they must do it themselves.

Most of us in human service professions want to repair damaged people, and professional ego trips are not uncommon. Yet the stark reality is that healing and repair take place within each person. A therapist or a friend may facilitate the healing process, but the individual has the potential, ability, and responsibility for the repair. Recognition of the need and willingness to forgive make repair possible.

Warning: Responsibility can be hazardous to your health

It is liberating to realize we are not responsible for the behavior of those who harm us. But the responsibility for being realistic, assessing the damage, and rebuilding ourselves can cause feelings of inadequacy and frustration. When too much is required from small children, they may give up, feeling inferior or ashamed. Adults may mirror these same feelings.

Realistically, contemplating the seriousness of deep hurts could put us in jeopardy of hating even more. A sense of powerlessness can weaken us. Squashed self-esteem is not therapeutic.

Understanding how someone has damaged us, we risk the possibility of magnifying our hatred toward those who have mistreated us. Getting bitter is not a rare experience.

Assuming responsibility for mending damage that the misconduct of others has caused is unfair and may make us acutely aware of our inability to control our lives and circumstances. Like children, we are apt to give up in shame.

But giving up only indicates immaturity, not inability. Toddlers may revert to crawling after a fall, but eventually they find walking a better way of locomotion. It is a major developmental task. The child who walks has access to toys and can navigate—especially when they climb—to places far beyond crawling peers. Walking opens new freedom and power for self-expression. But first the child must overcome the shame of a few tumbles.

To falter at accepting responsibility for our own emotional health is as normal as a toddler falling on his face. We may delay our first steps toward forgiveness. The little person must overcome his fear or wait for more psychomotor skills. But eventually he learns to walk.

However, immaturity is not a valid excuse when it comes to developing forgiveness skills. Emotional maturity and chronological age are not identical. We have no control over chronological age. Yet at any age, we can grow up emotionally, accept responsibility for ourselves, and mature into forgiving people. In emotional and spiritual areas of life, we have both choice and control. Immaturity and an unforgiving attitude need not be permanent personality traits.

Children are often fascinated with the idea that they are more mature than some adult authority figures. They delight in telling about immature attitudes and emotional infantilism they've observed in grown-ups. They enjoy comparing themselves with dysfunctional parents, teachers, and others who should know better. At times, children show more maturity than they get credit for. Often, they can analyze the fighting at home and suggest measures to correct it. A few could even be professors of education in colleges; perceptive enough to know how a teacher's emotional immaturity destroys professional competence, they could easily put order into a chaotic classroom.

It is exciting to see children grow into mature, responsible, forgiving human beings. They need not wait for further physical development to grow up emotionally; neither do we.

Risk is a part of life. We don't love without some risk of hurt and rejection. We take risks when we drive automobiles, jeopardizing life and health or damage to a new car. Routinely, we calculate those hazards that are worthwhile. For instance, polio vaccines are not without chance and a few individuals are aware of this. Yet the majority of us will never again fear that crippling disease. Some risks— even serious ones—are acceptable. The risk of ongoing, unrecognized, emotional malignancy is not.

CHAPTER III

Beginning with Self-Forgiveness

Love covers a multitude of sins—especially my own. But it's most difficult to forgive ourselves, much less love ourselves. Somehow we've been indoctrinated with the premise that loving ourselves is indecent—self-centered.

I grew up in a church where we sang, "... such a worm as I." Years later, the words were rewritten "... sinners such as I." I am a sinner, but I am not a worm. Sinners can be forgiven; worms are stuck with their ormness.

If we cannoake peace with another person, we can separate ourselves from that individual. Geographic distance can lower the heat of anger. Many people find sanctuary in a locked bathroom. Others move across the continent. However, we cannot escape from self. Jess Lair hinted at this in his book, *I Ain't Much Baby, But I'm All I've Got*.[1] We must live with ourselves wherever we are. There is no escape.

Forgiving ourselves is difficult but rewarding. Forgiving someone else does not guarantee a change in behavior nor is it a guarantee the person will not hurt us again. We are not responsible for the behavior of others. However, self-forgiveness is unique since we must assume responsibility for our own behavior. While we cannot change others, we can change ourselves.

Forgiving ourselves requires various degrees of emotional excavation. Acute anger like locking the keys in the car does not put our ego structure under microscopic analysis. A little patience will usually do the trick. On the other hand, self-depreciation or lack of self-esteem handicaps our lives and calls for a much deeper look into ourselves. A few guidelines may be helpful:

- *Negative feelings toward self are normal.* This does not relieve us of responsibility for self-control. We can find better ways to express bad feelings without hurting self.
- *We are human beings; human beings make mistakes.* This is not license for destructive behavior. Rather, it is a basis for self-compassion and patience. Human beings can change and do change. Self-forgiveness is an important avenue toward that goal.
- *We do not have to feel worthy to forgive ourselves.* That is why we deal with forgiveness rather than justice.
- *Forgiving ourselves is important preparation for forgiving others.* Choosing to love or hate ourselves influences how we see our environment and those who populate it.

CONQUERING EMOTIONAL INJURY AND FLATTENED SELF-ESTEEM
"I really had it coming."

Worthless but humble

As children, we were programmed to guard against an inflated ego. If we grew up in religious homes we were possibly subjected to well-intentioned but damaging attempts to make us humble. For instance, we were taught, "In sin did my mother conceive me," meaning we are despicable. We owe our existence to parents who were so base they could not refrain from being "nasty," that is, sexual.

Children often believed their parents "did it once" only for each offspring. They found it hard to imagine their parents "doing it" for any other reason than procreation. Deep inside, they suspected their parents may have really enjoyed "it" and worse yet, they felt an inner foreboding that some day they, too, could enjoy such depravity.

My father often quipped, "Everyone is good for something even if they only serve as a horrible example." Fortunately, worthlessness and humility are not synonymous. Humility requires a healthy concept of worth and potential and allows growth and development. Truly humble people recognize their personal deficits, but they are equally aware of their strengths. One can indeed be proud of humility if it is redefined to reflect a realistic appraisal of our value as a person. Humility is a means for self-development.

False piety, hidden behind a facade of humility and built on feelings of worthlessness, usually does not work well. It is frequently a cover of sanctity for malicious behavior.

Emotionally abusive homes are factories that turn out people who feel worthless. Emotional abuse is hard to identify and difficult to treat. In many homes, it seems normal and has gone on for generations. Parents protest, "That's the way my parents did it; it worked for me and I see no need to change!" So another generation fails to resolve anger, saves it, and eventually spews it out on their children.

Emotional maltreatment does not leave physical marks, but the psychological scars can disfigure a child's whole life. Over several years, I have collected examples of abusive barbs commonly inflicted on children. Imagine that you are five years old. This should be a good time in your life:

You are learning at a rapid rate.
You are discovering wonderful things about yourself.
You believe life is fun.
You get excited when Mommy and Daddy come home.

But fears trouble your young life. You sense something is wrong. Day in and day out those you love bombard you with:

- "You little dummy; I can't imagine a child being so stupid."
- "I don't have time for your nonsense; get the hell out of here."
- "I wish you had never been born."
- "Do that again and I'll slap the crap out of you."
- "We're getting a divorce because we can't stand your fussing."
- "You're a disgrace to our family."
- "You dirty little rat."
- "If you really love me, you'll stop driving me crazy."
- "If you don't stop lying, God will send you to hell."
- "If you hadn't worried your grandmother, she'd be alive today."
- "You're the one who causes the problems in this family."
- "You mess up more than you are worth."

Southern humorist, Lewis Grizzard, described the feeling in his book titled *They Tore Out My Heart and Stomped that Sucker Flat.*[2] Feeling flat and defeated, we tend to stay that way. We find our place, stake our claim, and spend the rest of our lives feeling inferior. There is no need to open doors; we slither under them. Self-esteem drops so low we need a stepladder to climb to hell.

When our sense of worth is crushed, we seek others who are equally desperate. We may attempt quasi-status with the attitude, "If I can't be the best at least I can be the worst." This attempt at repair can end in self-destructive competition. It is particularly harmful when young delinquents compete with one another to be the toughest or most antisocial.

Reversing this process is not easy. It begins with forgiving ourselves and rechanneling negative emotional energy into self-development. When self-esteem is low, it is nearly impossible to accept positive input from others. People who feel worthless believe affirmation from others is a signal that they will be used. Self-forgiveness equips us to accept genuine praise. Healthy humility helps us recognize we are worth forgiving, worth the effort to be a real person. A friend who was working on self-esteem once said, "You may not think I'm much, but you don't know where I started."

Love me; use me

The life of a sixteen-year-old girl was out of control and a court order placed her for treatment as her last hope. At fourteen she had a baby which she placed for adoption. The following year, she was pregnant again. She terminated this pregnancy by abortion. Failing to learn from experience, she suffered two episodes of sexually transmitted disease (STD). At the time of the referral she had been generous with the STD.

When she began therapy, she said she had to have sex with her boyfriends. She went on to explain that the boys told her they would get sick if their "balls got too full." Little did they realize they would soon be really sick. Sometimes there is justice. This young woman eventually got better, but not until she could forgive herself and allow herself to grow into a real person with worth and dignity.

Another promiscuous thirteen-year-old girl stormed into my office in a rage. Someone accused her of "acting like a whore." With fury in her voice she screamed, "I'm not a whore! I've never charged for it!"

Heartbreaking! She was a child looking for love but was unable to differentiate between love and being used. Her only claim to self-respect was giving away what prostitutes sell. Her quest for love was far more important than money. I have since heard her life is in shambles.

Without adequate self-esteem, it is easy to confuse sex and sexuality. Sexual intercourse is not only a unique expression of special love; it is also fun. Special nerve endings in the glans penis and clitoris have no known purpose other than pleasure. Biologically, two people who feel worthless can share a sense of mutual appreciation while using each other.

Young people with little or no self-esteem usually fail to establish standards for dates and mates. I often ask about their requirements. Popular answers among teenagers include "good looks" or "has personality." To clarify these responses, they often mention designer clothes or someone who "treats me nice." This can mean anything from "gives me money" to "slaps the hell out of me."

These unfortunate young people have no concept of qualities of character such as goal direction, personal responsibility, or investment of oneself in the welfare of another. One young man summarized his amorous feelings, telling his girlfriend, "I fuckin' love you!" She couldn't resist. They soon married.

Young men often believe that love and responsibility are separate entities. "Getting a piece of ass" is not the same as assuming responsibility for a meaningful relationship. To be "horny" has nothing to do with masculinity. For instance, a sixteen-year-old boy came to a group session, bragging that his girlfriend was pregnant. To his amazement, the group confronted him with his responsibility for her and the unborn child. He could reproduce, but he could not love.

The quest for love is carried into adult life. Like a mirage, happiness is always just ahead but out of reach. The search for "true love" may continue through one relationship after another. We confuse love and ownership. We can love an automobile and lavish it with considerable affection. But eventually, we sell or junk it. Despite intense feeling, this kind of love does not work well in relationships. Jealousy and ownership are attempts to hold unhealthy relationships together. To own is to use; to love is to cherish.

Loving and being loved is frightening and involves risk. We become vulnerable to rejection. Unselfish love requires too much and our loved one may prove so disappointing we cannot continue the relationship. Eventually, death breaks all relationships. No loving relationship is free from hurt. As a buffer, some couples mutually use each other. This does not eliminate pain, but it offers a fair amount of protection.

Conversely, the ability to forgive ourselves builds self-esteem. Self-esteem, in turn, builds strength, the strength that enables us to survive hurt. We learn to appreciate the value of who we are and what we can give in a relationship. Giving and receiving quality love is worth the price. We are too good to be used. We appreciate ourselves as a treasure we can share with another. As a worthy person, we are able to receive treasure of equal value and are unwilling to settle for less.

Fear of loneliness

Loneliness may be the most desolate of all feelings. I was taught that God created humankind to fill a need for companionship. This may be an extreme measure, but loneliness leaves an extreme emptiness. When we consider that God would not live in loneliness, it becomes easier to understand this intense fear in ourselves even though I don't understand God that well.

Loneliness is not natural. In much of life, we reach out to others. If healthy contact is not available, unhealthy contact serves as a substitute. When we do not love ourselves or have close proximity to someone else, we are without love—either real or artificial.

Several years ago I was touched deeply by the profound loneliness of a seven-year-old child who was tragically rejected. With hesitation, she handed me the following note:

To Dr. Schell.
From R.

Love is love for happy people. No one talked to me on Valentine's day. No one gave me a card. No one helped me. No one did nothing for me. They was doing their own thing. So I went home I hope you still love me.

Love, R.
If you don't mind.

In some areas, fifty to eighty-five percent of all births are to single mothers. Most of these infants are born to lonely teenage girls who are desperate for love. Some of these young women have told me they became pregnant intentionally. Paternity is no concern other than a source of sperm. A baby makes her feel important—loved. In many high schools, having a baby or two or three is a status symbol—a rite of passage into what is perceived as adulthood. It is insurance against loneliness. After all, a newborn is totally dependent. In truth, the infant is doing more for the emotionally deprived mother than she is doing for the baby.

Lonely people become embittered. Ironically, they see bitterness as a curative and bitter people have a way of finding one another. There is a perverse pleasure in reinforcing each other's bitterness in mutual, protracted bitch sessions. One easily becomes addicted to complaining. Caustic people usually have a caustic circle of friends. To change, they would risk loneliness.

Moving toward a sense of self-esteem can cause consternation. The question arises, "What if I change and nobody likes me?" This is a legitimate question because the risk of loneliness is real. To be sure, when we no longer allow others to control us, they may become angry and walk out of our lives.

Forgiving ourselves lifts self-esteem. We no longer need to tolerate abuse, negativism, or bitterness for companionship. As self-esteem grows, healthier people enter our lives. This, nevertheless, can be disturbing because we don't know how to relate to quality people. One must remember that mature people are not perfect; they will need forgiveness from time to time. However, they are more apt to forgive when the shoe is on the other foot.

Fly with eagles or flop with turkeys

Eagles are symbolic of freedom and strength. Turkeys, on the other hand, become sandwiches the day after Thanksgiving. In human terms, eagles succeed at their jobs, have happy homes and good friends, and tend to be leaders. In contradistinction, turkeys look continuously for happiness but don't understand how to make it happen. Eagles live; turkeys exist. Eagles are active and build life. Turkeys are passive and look to others to build life for them. Eagles assume responsibility for their circumstances and the direction of their lives. Turkeys create clever excuses for their self-defeating lives. Eagles are in control; turkeys are controlled.

Lifestyles, set early in life, resist change. Fortunately, people can and do change, but it takes much work and practice. A lifestyle of bitterness grows out of ingrained hostility. Nevertheless, people can become better.

Turkeys may appear to be successful and in control, but they are not at peace with themselves or with those who love them. For instance, workaholics look successful. Yet compulsive work habits are usually attempts to resolve internal, unrealized conflicts which inhibit quality relationships. Work replaces intimacy.

The differences are important. Basic turkey attitudes are incompatible with the eagle lifestyle. A hostile or passive posture will not contribute to personal emotional development. Eagles are not exempt from problems or abuse, but they recover and become stronger in the process.

Initial programming for eaglehood or turkeydom begins soon after birth, but adolescence is a particularly important time for deciding roles in life. Eagles are most often career oriented, make good grades, and associate with sharp people. Turkeys attend school because they have to. They hope for good jobs but are inept in the pursuit of a goal.

True, turkeys are impulsive and may have more fun. Teenage turkeys enjoy drugs, alcohol, and sex while eagles laboriously do homework. Some turkeys are remarkably intelligent. A few have indicated they can make more money on the streets than I can in my profession. They are right. Some are in the fast lane to nowhere with a full tank of gas.

Turkeys are emotionally stunted people. Turkey behaviors are attempts to overcome their perceived inadequacies and to compensate for loss of self-esteem. They hope their frustrations will just go away. They don't understand that negative feelings convert into bitterness which grows more intense as life progresses. They discern forgiveness as weakness.

Eagles, of course, are not exempt from anger and frustration but they have confidence and make healthy resolutions. They assume responsibility for their own emotional maturity. As inwardly strong people, they forgive others without being threatened. To them, forgiveness is a sign of strength.

Teenagers live in a strict social caste system. Eagles fly with eagles; turkeys flop with turkeys. The caste is rigid and is evident in any high school. Birds of a feather do flock together. Teen pressure is overwhelming. Parents who fail to recognize how destructive peers in the turkey flock can be are likely busy raising a second generation of gobblers.

The metamorphosis from turkey to eagle is difficult, not only for adolescents but is also a monumental task for anyone. Fortunately, turkeys have good survival skills which they may use to build rather than destroy. They need to exert a willingness to step out and associate with eagles. Real eagles will understand and appreciate the effort. Courage to forgive is vital to overcome the bitterness that keeps one cooped up on the turkey farm. The choice is solely one's own.

OVERCOMING NEEDLESS GUILT
AND POOR EMOTIONAL HYGIENE
"Don't worry about me; no one cares anyway."

Thank God for guilt

Because guilt hurts, it can, at times, contribute to serious emotional illness. Drugs, alcohol, and medication have no effect on guilt. It can play a haunting refrain that lingers throughout life, driving us to despair. When psychotherapy fails to meet guilt head-on, it helps little more than a side-saddle on a pig.

In the therapeutic process, it is necessary at times to increase guilt rather than assuage it. For instance, a hostile fourteen-year-old boy became so angry at his mother that, as he screamed at her, "Shut your goddamn mouth!" he picked up a lamp and hit her.

When this incident emerged in his next therapy session, he laughed as his mother tearfully recited the fracas. He took the opportunity to chastise her, saying she had deserved the treatment and had no right to make him get off the telephone. He added, "And, old woman, you had better never touch me again!" He delighted in the revenge of this newly discovered power over her. She melted in defeat.

At this point, I intervened with strong therapeutic confrontation. Risking injury to myself, I forced him to determine whether his behavior was right or wrong. He made numerous excuses which I debunked as "bullshit." His future depended on his ability to control his own behavior. For too long, folks had allowed him to make excuses for his conduct rather than discipline him. He continued his campaign to blame his family, environment, school, neighborhood. I continued to disallow his excuses and pressed him to judge the right or wrong of cursing and hitting his mother. Finally, he dissolved in tears and sobbed, "I know down inside I was wrong."

Although this experience did not cure everything, it was a turning point. He found guilt, and guilt became his friend.

We need not fear guilt. It is a natural, though powerful, experience. Too much guilt can, of course, stymie emotional maturity. But failure to experience normal guilt is a serious symptom among antisocial personalities such as psychopaths, sociopaths, or criminal personalities. Hospitals are full of people with too much guilt; jails are full of those with too little guilt.

When guilt is healthy, it signals the need to correct behavior and to forgive ourselves. It is like a fever signaling an infection. Fever fights off intruders in the bloodstream. Too much fever may cook the brain but too little lets the infection rage on.

To avoid guilt, some attempt to blame God or some other moral standard. But guilt is a personal experience; full responsibility rests with the individual. For instance, to disregard the Ten Commandments is usually an effort to justify behavior without dealing with moral issues.

Mitigating moral structure is an artificial attempt to lessen guilt. Many young people believe morality is a disease the Puritans brought to America. Without morality, guilt has no meaning.

At a seminar I was conducting for public school teachers, I shared my views on the need to teach moral concepts as an integral part of total education. Immediately, the attendees informed me that teaching right or wrong is not the domain of public education. They explained the risk of putting themselves in jeopardy should they undertake to do so. I quickly responded that teachers take swift action if a student is caught cheating on an exam, stealing a teacher's purse, or putting another student in danger. What they really meant was that teachers were fearful about teaching sexual morality, dealing with such issues as birth control, abortion, and single parenthood. No wonder young people are confused.

Some parents have developed a moral phobia complete with panic attacks at the thought of teaching their children values, ethics, and personal responsibility. They break into a cold sweat at the idea of being labeled old-fashioned. Only the valiant teach morality.

Parents complain that they don't have time to teach morality. The complaint is valid but moral retardation is preventable and reversible in its early stages. Careers and parenthood are hard to balance. Latch-key children are left to their own devices to learn life. Children may learn sophisticated academic subjects, but intelligence and morality are not the same. As a matter of fact, education may only give one more power to exercise immorality. I am mildly amused when I hear the term, "good doctor." Some are mean as hell.

Children receive far too much moral teaching passively from television. This is controversial, but those of us who work on the frontlines with impressionable children know how powerful mass communication is in influencing moral development. Take time to observe the violence children view. Even benevolent cartoons are not so benevolent. They are filled with hitting people, putting others down, argumentative communication, and destruction. There is little regard for the rights and the value of other persons. But children's media has one socially redeeming feature—kids love it and that sells a lot of cereal. This, in turn, is good for the economy.

One of my nine-year-old TV addicts got into trouble for clotheslining, his term for hitting another child across the throat with the back of his forearm. He told me he had learned to target the "Adam's apple" and eliminate (knock down) other kids. He had no qualms about hurting a child who was taken to the emergency room with throat constricture. After that incident, we worked on feeling appropriate guilt.

Another ten-year-old expert at clotheslining asked his mother if he could take karate lessons. When she asked my professional advice on the matter, I gave it: "No! Hell no!"

When are we going to learn the value of other human beings? To hurt others physically or emotionally without guilt is sick. It is very sick.

Guilt has an important purpose: it regulates behavior. Without guilt we would never feel the need to forgive ourselves and get better. Self-forgiveness is the only cure for guilt. Thank God for healthy guilt; it keeps us between the ditches.

Guilty for feeling guilty

A dear friend recently said, "I'm guilty if I'm late; I'm guilty if I drive too fast." Most of us can identify with the feeling. Guilt is healthy until it runs amok.

As children, feeling shame, fear, and guilt controlled most of us. But this control also brought a sense of security. We felt safe when someone else took over and told us how we should feel. This was particularly valuable when life was in chaos, a normal state of affairs in many homes.

Moving into adult life, we are driven by the winds of fear, shame, and guilt. We use them to navigate us through life. When our parents no longer manipulate us as children, we search for others who will take over the job. Without shame, fear, and guilt we may feel becalmed at sea—stranded. We fear dying alone.

To forgive those who have ruthlessly controlled our emotional guilt buttons is to risk living without steerage. But first, we must forgive ourselves for allowing them to assume command. No one can mash our guilt buttons unless we permit it.

Children who have been controlled by guilt find themselves in an endless search for approval. Elderly people may search for parental approval decades after their parents have died. Young and old may have no idea why they feel so guilty or who they should forgive.

Children often feel better after they are punished. Many of us undertook an endless quest of making atonement only to find that we were never good enough. At least punishment brought temporary relief. Someone cared enough to punish even if it was too severe. Without really knowing why, someone usually caught us for minor infractions. When we were not caught, we eventually told on ourselves. Punishment felt so good.

Today, as adults, we look to others to continue punishing us. Self-defeating domestic relationships—especially when they are abusive—serve this purpose well.

Needless guilt is guilt bereft of reason. It becomes self-destructive. We experience anger toward ourselves and this, in turn, produces more guilt. We have successfully achieved perpetual motion.

Suicidal people, often caught up in needless guilt, see no way out—no hope for relief. They believe no one cares and they, therefore, cannot accept caring. Having learned to hate themselves, they cannot accept love from others. A girl, thirteen years old, wrote:

> When I was at home, the problem that we had was hell. Most of the time there wasn't nothing going on but sex and beating. Soon I just got fed up with the shit. One time I started to hit my father, but I knew I would be in trouble.

Three years later, after being hospitalized many times for psychiatric care, she was still unwilling to forgive herself. She wrote:

> I am afraid to be put back into the hospital ... my biggest thing is having to be guilty or take on guilt.

In another letter she wrote:

> I know that some of the feeling will never go away.... The only way this could end, I would have to kill myself. I don't want to end it this way, but that is the only way.

She continues to exist as an adult but she is unable to lay aside needless guilt. She has assumed guilt which, in fact, belongs to others. Agony is never far away. The crimes of those who should have loved her have damaged her ability to experience normal guilt. She knows healing will come only when she forgives herself—and them.

Abnormal guilt is used in dysfunctional marriages in an attempt to control each other. "If you loved me, you would not have done it." "You should have known how I felt." "If you really cared, I wouldn't have to tell you." Such statements are efforts to inflict blame for failing to read the other's mind. It is surprising how often these guilt trips work.

Distress over being angry at God is another anxious form of guilt. One seldom acknowledges this pain. Few people are honest enough with themselves to admit anger at God. Yet we humans do not always understand or agree with the course of his creation. At times, we may doubt that he cares at all. This is particularly true when we see the suffering of innocent children who cannot protect themselves.

I recall a brave, honest woman whose small son had been attacked by a cruel adult. Not only was she angry at the perpetrator, she also felt guilty for being angry at God for allowing it to happen. Eventually, her deep faith helped her to realize that God would understand her need to forgive him. She recovered from this shattering trauma and from needless guilt. She forgave both the perpetrator and God. Her faith—and mine—grew in the process.

There is no therapeutic value in needless self-blame. Undeserved self-recrimination has no virtue. Self-forgiveness is the only antidote for guilt. To overcome bitterness and become better people without first forgiving self is like spitting into the wind.

Making peace with our past

To be sure, we must forgive others who have hurt us. But to experience peace with the past, we must forgive our own mistakes. Forgiving the past includes forgiving our complicity in shaping it. Peace with the past instills hope for the future.

An elderly man asked for help after his wife threatened to leave him. She complained that he had been a tyrant for over forty years, ruling the family with relentless rigidity. She challenged him with two choices: become more flexible or live without her for the rest of his life.

Because he truly loved his wife and treasured their relationship, he entered therapy. At first he made progress, but setbacks became more frequent. His wife became increasingly frustrated.

One day he went to his therapist in a lighthearted mood. As in other sessions, he explored various areas of his childhood. Suddenly his demeanor changed. His face flushed and the dam broke. In a healthy catharsis of tears, he related that his mother had abandoned him as a child. He didn't know his father. An aunt tried to provide a home, but she had a life of her own and it did not include him. He grew up working for room and board on one farm after another and dreamed of someday having a better life.

Through hard work and determination, he eventually built a career and had a family with several children. For years he was a good provider, but his dictatorial manner robbed him of the emotional fulfillment he so desperately needed. At last, he realized he had been so afraid of losing his family that he had abused them. He used his despotic control to prevent them from leaving him like his mother and aunt had done.

Forgiving his mother and his aunt was a major accomplishment, but it was not complete until he forgave himself. Aside from forgiving those who had deserted him as a child, he found the need to forgive himself. After deep inward searching, he forgave his unwillingness to forgive as well as the years of his cruel behavior. Forgiveness offers no guarantees other than inward peace, but in this case, the man salvaged his marriage and relationship with his now adult children. As an additional benefit, he found new meaning in his grandchildren. He learned late—but not too late.

To deny or distort the reality of our past is not healthy. Psychosis is basically separation from reality. To reshape the past mentally in order to live with it is crazy. Guilt, depression and bending reality may appear easier than forgiveness. Like electricity, most of us take the course of least resistance. But in doing so, we short-circuit forgiving our past and become progressively bitter.

Forgiveness is not the course of least resistance. To face the past may hurt. Confession to ourselves, others, or God is often beneficial. Therapeutic support from others—spiritual resources and trusted confidants are valuable reservoirs of support—can help to avoid glossing over mistakes while encouraging self-directed compassion and forgiveness. After all, if someone else can forgive our past, maybe we can forgive it too.

Self-forgiveness involves a change in attitude toward ourselves. This results in changing how we treat ourselves. By practicing self-discipline, we can reject needless guilt and feel better. We no longer need to torture ourselves with cruel reminders of past embarrassments and misbehaviors that others have long forgotten.

Peace with our past may be unfamiliar turf, and we don't know how to begin shaping the future. Responsibility for growth can be burdensome. But making peace with the past helps us learn from mistakes as opposed to having them stunt us. This makes good building material.

When we forgive the past, we are no longer emotionally shackled to it and those self-defeating hours of replaying traumatic errors like worn-out movies come to an end. We no longer use the present to lament the past but to plan for the future.

Free at last

No prisons are more confining than those we build for ourselves. Self-punishing behaviors range from rejecting compliments to involvement in destructive relationships, to drug or alcohol addiction, to suicide. All are symptoms of self-hate and self-imposed incarceration.

An intelligent young woman shared how she had ruined her health, becoming addicted to cocaine. For years she wanted to free herself from her parents. She experienced a deep self-loathing emanating from childhood feelings of rejection. Cocaine and counterculture friends gave her a sense of being free. She felt liberated from self-depreciation. In reality, she built a prison complete with torture rack.

Children of divorced parents are often locked in prisons of guilt. Smaller children often believe they are at fault for their parents' separation. One little boy said if he had "stayed home from school that awful day," he could have kept his parents together. Fortunately, there is help for most of these children. With the parents' cooperation, the children get the assurance that it is their parents and not themselves who are divorced, and that it is not disloyal to love both parents. This eases their pain. It also increases the odds that they will forgive the parents, which makes it easier for parents to forgive themselves.

Post-divorce hatred is a common way to be chained to hostility. All divorces are traumatic, but divorce has a purpose. When the gavel falls, hostilities should cease. Unhappily, most people do not allow their divorces to work any better than their marriages—especially when children are involved. The family continues living in a war zone, but the stakes are higher. Vendettas become more serious and the couple uses the children as pawns. "You are as worthless as your father," or "You are selfish like your mother's family," are subtle attempts to manipulate children into hating the other parent.

Managed in this fashion, children soon learn to control their parents. They pit one parent against the other for favor and usually accumulate things that the guilt-ridden adults offer as appeasement. They circumvent parental authority and get privileges without responsibility. Playing on the mutual guilt and hatred of their parents, they become undisciplined. Seeking freedom from restraint, they become prisoners in their own insecurity.

Guilt no longer controls divorced parents who forgive themselves, and they restore healthy parental authority. Those who forgive themselves not only free their children, but they also liberate themselves to forgive the other parent. Forgiveness is not synonymous with marital reconciliation although any attempt at reconciliation without forgiveness is only an exercise in futility.

In forgiving ourselves, we issue our own Emancipation Proclamation. Freedom might be frightening, but no longer is there a need to punish ourselves, hoping to pay for our mistakes. We are free from the compulsion to judge ourselves harshly and we can channel that energy into self-evaluation and personal growth.

Healthy new attitudes emerge with personal freedom and unfamiliar but exciting avenues of thinking, feeling, and behaving open up. Self-respect becomes a reality; it is no longer contingent on the approval of others.

With liberation and newfound self-respect comes the responsibility to protect ourselves and freedom to stand up for ourselves. But care needs to be taken lest we react in an abusive way. Retaliation signals incomplete forgiveness.

Forgiving ourselves frees us to be assertive, not antagonistic. We are free to guard our personage from assault but it is not open season to attack those who have abused us. In extreme cases, we may need legal protection from those who could hurt us. But that protection should be motivated by self-respect rather than by a desire to punish offenders, even though they deserve to suffer.

LEARNING TO LOVE OURSELVES AND FEELING GOOD ABOUT IT
"Maybe I'm not so bad after all."

Snobs vs. slobs

No one seems to know for sure what a snob is. Some suggest it means "snobody;" others speculate it comes from the Latin *sine nobilis*—"without nobility." Most people equate it with being "uppity"—an artificial self-aggrandizement. Given a choice, it's easier to be a slob. A slob doesn't pretend or expend energy on self-improvement. While a snob invests nothing toward personal growth, it requires a great deal of work to keep up the image.

In a democratic society there is an emphasis on all being created equal. In reality, most of us tend to recreate ourselves in a fashion that makes us feel inferior or superior to others. Inferiority complexes are far more common than the superiority brand. Both are false perceptions and symptomatic of self-disdain.

Snobs and slobs don't get along very well. Snobs snub slobs; slobs snub snobs. The cycle goes on and no one gets better. Slobs view self-improvement as taking on snobhood. Snobs view slobs as weak and inept.

Sociologists refer to an individual's place in the structure of society as "social location." Most of us were programmed early to "know your place." We were taught, "Don't get smart with me," but we were expected to make good grades. We were told, "Don't be a big shot," but were pressed toward upward mobility. We were taught, too, to associate only with certain groups or classes of people.

Nowhere is social strata more evident than among teenagers. High schools are microcosms of society at large. One southern high school has preppies, cowboys, and rednecks. To move from one level to another is nearly impossible. Personal worth has little value. Only conformity to a recognized group of cohorts carries any clout.

To have a healthy love of self, it is necessary to rise above the narrow structures of social stigma. Self-forgiving, mature people don't need to put others down to make themselves look better.

Artificial airs are attempts to relate to others without revealing self. This is insulation against rejection from those who get too close or make us feel inferior. We can snub them before they snub us.

Refusing to forgive ourselves tends to drive others away and relieves us from having to make social adjustments. Self-hating, embittered people may have many superficial acquaintances but few have deep relationships. Shying away from others is likely when we are unable to manage feelings of guilt and inferiority. Without self-forgiveness, snobbery and slobbery are routine reactions.

To love ourselves requires self-forgiveness. It is beyond the immaturity of snobbery or slobbery. Genuine love of self does not belittle or exhibit conceit. Rather, it is a major step toward becoming a person we can honestly respect.

Self-forgiveness resolves self-hate and we see ourselves as we actually are without being crushed in despair. Mistakes are reparable and snobbery or slobbery becomes a useless mechanism.

Mother, may I?

A nine-year-old boy loses all interest in living; a six-year-old boy wants to die; a thirteen-year-old girl attempts to take her own life. These are children who feel they are not special to anyone. Many such children are indeed special to someone. Yet, they do not sense this warmth of being loved for their own uniqueness.

The importance of parental approval is often apparent in children's games. The game "Mother, may I?" tests each participant's skill to get approval no matter how insignificant the behavior.

Children need to feel special. In early infancy, neglected neonates may not thrive. Later, children become passive or belligerent in their attempts to get special attention. Lying, stealing, bedwetting, school failure, and a host of other symptoms are common attention-seeking behaviors.

Teenagers may gravitate toward delinquency, sexual acting out, or drug and alcohol abuse. These behaviors offer instant acceptance among a noncritical peer group that gives the illusion of feeling special.

Ideally, feeling special should begin early in life. Babies have a right to be welcomed into the world with celebration. Parents and family members should receive and appreciate each child as an individual. They are in a unique position to provide the quality of love the child needs to feel special.

The love of parents is especially important and contributes to a developing child's sense of personal security, dignity, and self-worth. If parents don't encourage self-worth, children are left without parental approval or permission to love themselves and be real people. They become adults and attempt to fill the void by playing a perverted form of the children's game, "Mother, may I?" Sadly, the void is never filled, but the game goes on.

Some youngsters never experience parental approval or love. A few become so pathologically enmeshed with their parents that they can't answer even a simple question without looking to their parents for permission to speak. Others cast their eyes toward the parents expecting them to answer for them. These unfortunate children feel they don't have permission to exist, much less to forgive or love themselves.

Occasionally, some of these emotionally stunted youngsters will accept my permission as a surrogate authority to love themselves. Ultimately, they must grant this permission to themselves and become autonomous individuals with or without parental love or approval.

Parental approval is essential for the emotional development of children, but such approval is not a matter of survival for adults. Grown-ups have the right to grant self-approval and permission to love themselves.

It isn't likely that we ever outgrow the need for the approval of others. Of course, we cannot always please everyone. Yet, we work hard at being liked. After all, we're among the nicest of people. In spite of this, a few people seem to loathe us. I once quipped that the negative reactions of others toward me were deeply disturbing until I realized that if I were someone else, I would want me for a friend. Those who despise me are missing a beautiful friendship.

Some view self-approval as conceit, but if we offer approval to others, why not offer it to ourselves. Forgiving ourselves enables us to look beyond our errant behavior and love the person we are.

Learning to love ourselves leads to new heights of self-confidence and respect. A child looks to parents for physical and emotional protection. However, as adults, we assume the responsibility to protect ourselves. This, of course, does not mean we counterattack those who mistreat us.

A likable thirty-five-year-old man suddenly became verbally abusive and abrasive. Social and family relationships came crashing down. After some time, he admitted that he had attended an assertiveness workshop and was merely attempting to assert himself. This new freedom was dangerous. With some guidance, this man gave himself permission to be assertive rather than abusive—and he liked himself better.

Many of us never received parental permission to get angry; consequently, we suffered disapproval and guilt for normal feelings. Children see adults express anger but, regarded as second- or third-class human beings, they are not allowed the same privilege.

Adults have an internal parent and an endless "Mother, may I?" is not necessary for parental approval. The mature internal parent is perfectly capable of granting permission to love and forgive.

Making peace with ourselves

While a student in graduate school, I learned one of the most important lessons of my life in an unusual way. It was a beautiful day with bright sunshine and a refreshing breeze. I drove onto the causeway—one of the longest bridges in the world—and headed for my home in New Orleans. As I traveled along, I began thinking about graduation and finally being free from the rigors of my present program of study. But what if I washed out? What if my dissertation was rejected? What if I failed my oral defense? My blood ran cold at the thought of a committee flushing years of hard work down the drain. Without realizing it, I was driving in a rage, a menace to myself and to everyone else on the causeway.

The thought suddenly occurred to me: I had started the journey on a beautiful day, feeling great. I was nearing the end in anger and rage. I didn't give a damn about the sunshine or cool breeze; it was a lousy day.

Then, like a flash of lightning, I realized I was alone in the car. There was no one to blame for my anger. I had caused my own misery. In reality, my professors were far more interested in teaching than in failing me. Each one had been supportive and helpful. My fury was inside myself. Furthermore, since I was solely responsible for my agony, only I could resolve it.

Approaching the end of the causeway, I made a life-changing decision. I was tired of my own bitterness; I no longer wanted to be a hostile person. The hostility was only hurting me. I stopped the car and walked along the shore of Lake Pontchartrain. There I signed a peace pact with myself. It was a beautiful day, the sun was shining, a refreshing breeze was blowing.

Making peace with ourselves opens new dimensions. The war within is over. We accept ourselves and begin practicing love and forgiveness.

In a war with ourselves, self-condemnation and harsh judgment are cruel weapons that inflict misery. Peace allows us to judge our intentions rather than our actual behavior. Granted, we should work to correct behavior, but we can come to appreciate our more noble intentions. For instance, when I complimented a woman on her new hairstyle, she broke into tears. She hated the new style and thought I was making fun of her. My intentions were good; my behavior inflicted pain. She judged my behavior; I judged my intentions. I was embarrassed but was at peace.

When we make peace with ourselves, we no longer need the approval of others. A friend once said, "Perhaps no one else can forgive me, but I can forgive myself." He went on to explain that he could attempt to repair whatever hurt or damage he caused, but he could not force anyone to forgive him. He learned that self-respect and personal peace are not contingent upon anyone else.

Making peace with ourselves changes our language. We delete put-downs, we learn to accept honest compliments and make honest statements. We allow ourselves to say, "I do my job well," or "I feel good about my parenting skills," or "I have a lot of love to give." Most of us can list far more negative than positive personal characteristics. We may hesitate to say good things about ourselves lest it sound like bragging. But when we are at peace with ourselves, we can accept our positive attributes, knowing they are true.

Hostile people don't like themselves very much. Others don't like them either. Making peace with ourselves helps us become more loving people. One eighteen-year-old man tried to take his life after his girlfriend went out with someone else. At war with himself, he could not lash out at her so he turned the hurt inward. We began working on inner peace. One day he laughed and exclaimed, "I wouldn't die for her if my life depended on it!" I hope he never loses that peace.

Self-forgiveness calms the soul and peace follows easily. The stage is set to extend love and forgiveness to others.

Love is for sharing

A lovely fifty-five-year old woman sought help for her late-in-life preteen daughter. She complained that the girl's grades were dropping, she refused to keep her room clean, and showed chronic disrespect for adult authority.

After a few sessions with mother and daughter together, their communication skills improved. Soon her grades were up to earlier standards. Her room hadn't improved much, but it was within normal limits, and she was exhibiting the manners her mother had taught her.

Expecting to end the sessions, we discussed it together. The daughter was ready, but the mother seemed to panic. She wanted to come alone for the next appointment.

During the next session, this articulate but nervous woman poured out her heart. She shared how she met and married her husband, a gentle, understanding man. She loved him deeply but, somehow, the marriage was flawed. During therapy, she realized her daughter sensed the strain in their marriage and thus felt insecure in the home.

We explored these feelings and began to focus on the quality of love in this home. She revealed she had grown up in an emotionally impoverished, somewhat abusive family where put-downs and criticism were the primary modes of discipline and control. She had never felt secure in love. Although she had much love to give, she had never been able to love herself. Feeling unworthy, she couldn't believe her husband or anyone else could love her.

Learning to forgive and love herself changed her life. She accepted her husband's love, a love which had always been there. She could also appreciate more fully the love she gave to this man.

Preventing the agony this woman experienced is an exciting feature of working with children. Children are entitled to a rich heritage of love. It is our way of sharing inner peace. I have found the following guidelines helpful for parents.

- *Show and tell.* Well-meaning parents often make the mistake of assuming that children automatically know parents love them. Others err in thinking that children get too old to be assured of parental affection. Even adults flourish emotionally when love is expressed. Children grow on hugs and words of parental approval.

- *Learn to praise*. Most parents find praise difficult and criticism easy. Yet children who hear only criticism are emotionally abused. Human beings seem to learn more and learn faster in a climate of praise and acceptance. Full benefit comes when praise is genuine, even for small accomplishments.
- *Recognize the child's accomplishments*. Various developmental accomplishments mark every stage of life. For instance, children learn to walk, talk, eat, dress themselves, read, write, socialize, earn a living, and eventually become independent adults. Each of these steps provides observant parents with opportunities to help youngsters feel special.
- *Cultivate special memories*. Children are usually fascinated with family photograph albums. Invariably, they search for pictures of themselves. Family photos are an effective way to help each child feel loved and special. A section designated for each child is an affirmation of the youngster's place in the hearts of those who love him. Oral traditions telling about a child's birth or other special events also reinforce that wonderful feeling of being special and worthy of love.

Loving ourselves enables us to make more loving responses to others. We set a foundation for becoming a loving person. People who have a healthy foundation of love for themselves tend to act lovely. Thus a chain reaction develops. Those who act lovely attract other lovely people and lovely people are forgiving people. Building material is plentiful. Preventing bitterness is the best way to betterness.

Appropriate self-love is essential for personal maturity. A biblical narrative comes to mind. A group of malcontents was arguing with Jesus when a lawyer steps up and asks him which is the most important commandment. The lawyer challenges Jesus to reduce volumes of laws written over centuries to a single statement. In reply, Jesus cites the ancient Shema teaching that one should love God with all the heart, soul, and mind. Then he offers an unsolicited second commandment: "You shall love your neighbor as yourself."[3]

If I hate myself and love my neighbor in the same way, we are not likely to get along. If I am suicidal and love my neighbor in likemanner, I might kill him. Worse yet, what if my neighbor hates himself?

Love is for sharing. Forgiving ourselves makes it meaningful.

CHAPTER IV

Becoming a Forgiving Person

A thirty-eight-year-old father of four found his life in a state of emotional malignancy three years after his wife took their children and deserted him. At the time of their divorce, he settled in court. He agreed to sell their home and turn the capital over to her for the youngsters. In addition, he willingly paid generous child support. Helplessly, he watched his ex-wife deplete their life's savings on drugs and alcohol while she neglected the children. Time and again the courts rejected his pleas for custodial reconsideration, stating that "children are better off with their mother."

Eventually her neglect became so serious that the children were taken from her and he finally gained custody. In the interim, he had become a bitter, broken man. After some time, he realized forgiveness was his only hope for emotional survival. He entered therapy, talked to supportive friends, and searched his soul, but he had little or no relief.

Gradually, he experienced a breakthrough. He realized that, although he had forgiven his wife, the hurt was still there. He discovered healing isn't as rapid as forgiving. This discovery renewed his determination to get better.

In achieving forgiveness, wounds can be kept clean and healing is possible. Sterile wounds do not fester easily. This courageous father found his way and he got better. More significantly he blazed a trail for building character which his children now follow.

This man blazed his own trail but many of us need a trail to follow. Some claim that forgiveness is a spontaneous experience. What a wonderful experience! But sometimes the claim, "It just went away," really means the person has pushed the anger deeper inside where it lurks to reemerge in a disguised form. Yet, there are those rare individuals who forgive naturally. They make the world a better place.

Several of my colleagues question whether forgiveness is a single act (punctiliar) or a process (linear). This is a matter of individual perception and experience with advantages and disadvantages to each view.

Forgiveness as a punctiliar experience is swift and decisive, but it risks avoiding in-depth exploration of feelings. As a linear process, forgiveness encourages deeper introspection; it risks delay in dealing with emotionally gangrenous issues. Debating these concepts with my friends has been helpful, but the primary question remains: Has forgiveness actually taken place? A secondary but nonetheless important question is whether or not forgiveness is incorporated into our personalities.

When I conduct workshops or seminars on psychotherapeutic forgiveness, someone invariably asks for a presentation on "how to's." Understandably, specific "how to's" are extremely difficult; every person is different and each problem is unique. David Augsburger said, "True forgiveness is the hardest thing in the universe." [1] There is no simple way. However, once we overcome resistance and recognize the need to forgive ourselves, we are ready to take some definitive steps toward becoming a forgiving person. These are spotlighting the villain, gaining control over our anger, and climbing over the mountain.

SPOTLIGHT ON THE VILLAIN
"Making a list, checking it twice"

Working through our hit list

Generally, teenagers learn little from adults and even less from their parents. I was no exception to that generalization. However, I recall at least one important lesson I learned from my father. As a thirteen-year-old maladapted student, I was sure that a certain school administrator "had it in for me" and caused all of my problems. I was called to his office at any hint of trouble and sometimes unjustly accused and punished. I knew I was a better man than he because I hated him more than he could possibly hate me.

My father always reminded me that if I was in trouble at school, I was in trouble at home. I didn't expect sympathy from my parents, but my school problems were getting worse and my education was in jeopardy.

One evening my father came to my room. His tone of voice indicated he was serious. Calmly but firmly, he told me he had gone to school to talk to the administrator. Then came the surprise of my life. In his own words, Dad told me he found the administrator to be a petty, immature, unhappy person who was not likely to change. However, he assured the official that my behavior would improve. Dad went on to explain that acrimonious people are everywhere and often in positions of authority. Furthermore, he said the most important part of my education would not come from books but from learning to get along with people like the administrator.

Dad ended the lecture, saying simply, "He has more education than I do, but I think I am right." Dad was wrong at this point. When it came to understanding life, my father had far more education.

Putting this school official on my emotional hit list had not helped. It was only after I worked through my feelings that I got better. Having such a list is a prerequisite to working through it.

The late Dr. Harold Rutledge, professor of psychology and counseling at the New Orleans Baptist Theological Seminary, often said, "All human problems are created in the context of human relationships; therefore, all human problems are solved in the context of human relationships." We do not forgive situations; we forgive people. A hit list at least clarifies whom we need to forgive.

Coming up with a therapeutic list as opposed to a self-destructive, bitter hit list requires much thought. A therapeutic list helps to untangle emotional confusion. In addition, we might make a few notes about the damage these people have caused, the likelihood of their continuing the offense, and how we will deal with it.

After developing the list, it becomes necessary to change its nature and intent. Each item represents a specific need for emotional resolution and the achievement of a goal in the course of personal development. "Hit list" is a term associated with underworld figures who are targeted for assassination. As we work through our personal therapeutic list, it serves as a guide toward our being more forgiving and, as a result, better people.

When our list gets top-heavy

A sure way to recognize a top-heavy list is to realize that one person is the recipient of most of our hostility. Spouses often catch hell when the actual cause is job related. Children despise and blame teachers when they are really angry at parents.

My first observation was the unusually deep lines in her brow and the deep angles of her downturned mouth. I sensed an aura of anger about her. She looked much older than her forty-seven years.

She confirmed the chronicity of her anger in our first session. I was the eighth therapist she had seen in the last ten years. Shopping for the right doctor had become an obsession. She traveled to distant cities hoping for relief. Repeatedly, she accused her husband of being cold, uncaring, despicable, and emotionally cruel. Bitterly, she complained that he caused her over twenty-five years of suffering.

After consulting with several other previous therapists, I developed a composite picture of her treatment history. Her complaint had not changed in ten years.

I discovered that her husband was actually a pretty decent man, especially when one took into consideration the bitterness he had lived with. This woman had suffered disabling hostility long before their marriage. However, her spouse had become the exclusive object of her rage. Her list was top heavy.

Over a period of time she was able to readjust her list. Among others, she identified her parents along with an employer who had fired her long ago. When she concentrated her bitterness on only one person, it was too much to overcome. After discovering that her bitterness was the sum of many angers toward several people, she was able to work through each problem.

Of course, one has to take care to dilute hostility to manageable proportions. Adding to the list or updating it for the sake of accuracy helps to sort out feelings. But lengthening the list unnecessarily can multiply hostility.

Another caution is to believe that a top-heavy list is all-inclusive. We may forgive the person on top of the list without realizing there are others to forgive.

Top-heavy lists may also mask more generic bitterness. We become fixated on our hatred toward a single individual and ignore the damage others have inflicted on us. This cripples emotional growth when we neglect the need to deal with other malignant unrecognized issues.

When readjusting a top-heavy list, bear in mind that forgiving rotten people is permissible. We break no laws even if we choose to love them. After all, undeserving people need love too.

Realistically, there are times when the list is legitimately top-heavy. A mother and a father felt murderous hate toward the molester of their six-year-old daughter. Their feelings, though normal, were potentially dangerous. Many families break up after one member has been victimized. Hate, guilt, and vengeance do not contribute to healthy family development or healing. In these cases, a top-heavy list needs to be converted into a priority list. Forgiving such criminal behavior should take its rightful place at the very top.

Good guys wear white hats

Old western movies made life seem less complicated. Bad buys wore black hats; good guys wore white hats. But in real life, good people can do bad things and bad people are capable of good. This raises an old philosophical question: "Are people basically good and tend to be bad or are they basically bad and tend to be good?"

An attitude of unforgiveness can destroy our view of the world and make it easy to forget there are many wonderful people. If we become bitter, we will not be comfortable associating with people who are kind and compassionate. We may find ourselves ridiculing rather than emulating them.

Of course, good people do bad things, but that is not the real issue. We use their mistakes as an excuse to avoid forgiveness and personal growth. We feel justified in breaking a relationship with them. In a feeble effort to make ourselves feel better, we attempt to discredit their goodness by putting them down.

Hypocrites are particularly subject to critical scrutiny. Yet, hypocrites are special people and I take my position alongside them. I am a card-carrying hypocrite and actively campaign for more compassion, understanding, and appreciation. Hypocrites have rights too.

My definition of a hypocrite is one who has impeccable standards but lives at a lower level. The hypocrite, then, has a higher standard than he can achieve. To reach a lofty standard requires growth. It's a lifelong maturing process.

It's amusing to hear people complain of hypocrisy in the church. They level the charge that hypocrites live like saints on Sunday and like demons the rest of the week. But a church should be filled with hypocrites just as a hospital is filled with sick people. Trying one day a week is better than not trying at all—a step in the right direction.

Hypocrisy may be confusing, but internal bitterness may become so pervasive that we perceive everyone as evil, a potential or actual enemy. Sometimes we mistrust and tend toward paranoia. In extreme cases, contact with reality is lost, leading to psychosis.

Soldiers wear uniforms to distinguish friend from foe. In everyday life, though, our attitude determines friendliness or hostility. Bitterness and unforgiveness are generous with black hats. As we become more forgiving and less hostile, we realize that white hats are in style.

Giving up the blame game

Blame inhibits growth. If we can blame someone or some situation, we have no motivation for forgiving or changing. I became acutely aware of this several years ago when I worked with alcoholic men in a hospital. I discovered that most people begin drinking for good reasons, but when addiction takes place these reasons become twisted into irresponsible alibis. For instance, one man blamed his alcoholism on having hemorrhoids. Blame need not be valid to circumvent personal responsibility for forgiveness, healing, and growth.

As President Harry Truman said, "The buck stops here." Blame and responsibility can go no further. This applies to each of us. To be emotionally and spiritually healthy, we cannot continue to blame others or circumstances for our hurt and bitterness.

Expressing anger is often an attempt to control the uncontrollable. In frustration, we lash out with threats of violence hoping to force changes that may be impossible. When all else fails, we resort to blame. Forgiveness neutralizes anger, making blame unnecessary. The art of coping with the uncontrollable is succinctly summarized in the well-known but seldom practiced "Prayer of Serenity":

> God, grant me the serenity to accept the things I cannot change, the courage to change those things I can, and the wisdom to know the difference.

Sigmund Freud inadvertently made blame popular. The concept that atypical behavior is related to early nurturing (oral, anal, and genital stages) has implicated parents. Emotional disturbances and abnormal behaviors have been attributed to early parent/child relationships. Unfortunately, parents have been all too willing to accept the blame.

As a family therapist, I do not deal in blame. It is important to understand problems and recognize mistakes, but accusations and counter-accusations do not strengthen already shaky homes. Children quickly learn to press their parents' guilt buttons to gain control of the family. Couples and families get better when they stop blaming and start changing.

Blame cures nothing; forgiveness leads to healing. Yet, we don't relinquish blame easily. Often it is our last rationale for continuing crappy behavior.

Once we abandon the habit of blaming others, we must also learn to repudiate undeserved blame and forgive unmerited blame. Constructive criticism helps us profit from our mistakes. But mutual or unilateral blaming is a hostile game with no winners.

ANGER CONTROL
"I just can't do it!"

A better way to solve problems

The earlier a child learns to control anger, the easier the lesson. Early intervention is essential for the child, home, and civilization.

With rage in his voice, a three-year-old child picked up a building block and bashed it over the head of an unsuspecting playmate. His victim reacted by inflicting a savage blow to the face of her attacker. Fortunately, the building block was only cardboard designed for the safety of small children. Adult intervention terminated the hostilities and soon the two children were friends again.

Those familiar with the behavior of toddlers will recognize such occurrences as everyday routine. Younger children left without supervision can seriously injure one another since they lack restraint and basic impulse control.

As youngsters grow in body and mind, the potential for more serious violent behavior increases. Children in middle childhood have committed serious crimes including premeditated murder. Exposed to a constant diet of television violence, some children idolize violent heroes and make an effort to mimic their lifestyles. Others learn violence in their homes.

Teenage capacity for violence is frightening. Many, destined to populate penal institutions, experience their first entanglement in the judicial system during adolescent years. These youngsters are out of control, delinquent, or in need of supervision. A few express their inner hostility and frustration with weapons such as knives and guns. Clinicians identify them as exhibiting "adolescent antisocial behavior" or demonstrating a more chronic pattern known as a "conduct disorder" aggressive in nature. Simply, these labels describe young people who care little for the rights, feelings, or privileges of others. They view violence as a means of venting their rage and solving their problems.

Of course when teenagers become young adults, control over violent impulses is mandatory. They must abandon impetuous reactions of childish hitting, hurting, and fighting. Those who are unable to gain mastery over their behavior find violence wrecking their careers, marriages, and children. When they cannot achieve self-control, they are removed from civilized life and confined in barbaric prisons.

Few developmental tasks are as important as learning to control violent impulses. Failure to do so may destroy one's life as well as the lives of others.

Violence is frequently passed from one generation to the next. For instance, many parents who abuse their children were victims of abuse. Furthermore, statistics indicate that most prison inmates were abused or neglected during childhood.

Those who work with children generally agree that the earlier violent behavior problems are corrected, the more easily and quickly a child learns appropriate responses to frustration and distress. Older children and teenagers, however, may require more intensive treatment over a longer period of time with less hope for acceptable results.

Any child with a serious behavioral problem should get professional help. This is especially true when the child is apt to be violent. Parents, too, can do much to prevent serious problems by encouraging more acceptable forms of behavior. I have used the following guidelines for several years with good results:

- *Stop violent behavior immediately.* Children must learn that violence is inappropriate and will not be tolerated. Those who witness or practice violence in the home tend to become violent outside the home. Professional assistance becomes necessary when family violence gets out of control.

   Separating those in conflict can usually end less serious family violence, but severe violence may require police intervention. Violence signals loss of control and unless immediate steps are taken to halt home violence, these behaviors tend to escalate and become more destructive.

- *Teach rational problem solving skills.* Most violence erupts from unbridled emotion. Parents strike out at each other or their children and don't consider the consequences. They unwittingly teach their children that violence is the way to solve problems. Parents who beat others to express their anger need not be surprised when their offspring mimic their actions.

  Fortunately, parents can also teach youngsters to think before lashing out. A good form of discipline requires a child to describe in retrospect how he could have solved a problem without violence.

- *Demonstrate mature temper control.* Children learn self-control from their parents. Children who witness outbursts of temper may quickly imitate immature adult tantrums. Luckily, children learn maturity the same way.

  Explosive impulses are frightening for a child. Children find their own anger upsetting and feel insecure at the possibility of going out of control. Parents who model self-control by solving problems without violence help their youngsters become more emotionally secure.

- *Avoid an attitude of vengeance.* Some children learn early in life, by word or deed, that there is honor in vengeance. Of course, such thinking is absurd. The urge to retaliate when one is offended can lead to an endless succession of violent behaviors since there are always individuals who will treat us unfairly. Some particularly violent people seem to seek out situations which they believe require violent reprisals.

  Children need help in understanding that the sweet taste of revenge soon turns bitter while the practice of forgiveness builds character.

- *Develop respect and compassion for the feelings of others.* Children are basically selfish; they tend to remain selfish unless they are taught to care for others. Violence is symptomatic of a complete disregard for the feelings of people. To intentionally inflict emotional or physical pain on another human being violates the basic laws of human worth and dignity.

  The earlier children learn love, caring, and compassion, the easier it is to develop these qualities. Early acquisition helps these attributes to become permanent cornerstones in the growth of personal character.

Most children understand the need to outgrow the use of violence. Many respond to the challenge of learning to solve problems in more adult ways. Parents must provide leadership in this critical area.

If we were not taught anger control in childhood, we must attempt to teach ourselves. Smokey the Bear said, "Only you can prevent forest fires." This is true of emotional fires as well. In his book, *The Freedom of Forgiveness,* David Augsburger quoted Dr. William Menninger who wrote:

> Do not talk when angry. But after you have calmed down, do talk. Sometimes we push each other away and the problem between us festers and festers. Just as in surgery, free and adequate drainage is essential if healing is to take place.[2]

Some young people and adults consider a short temper a proud heritage: "I can't help it! My father and his father didn't take anything from anybody and neither will I." What a miserable way to live!

We are never exempt from attack and unfairness. This is largely out of our sphere of control. Fortunately, we can control how we respond to undeserved pain. Our first impulse is to strike back; this usually antagonizes and escalates conflict. When we learn better ways to solve problems, we become better people. Forgiveness meets that criteria.

Not long ago I was talking to my mother about learning new problem solving skills. She suggested that we can learn skills but they are useless unless we use them under the heat of attack and anger. She went on to remind me that a rational soft answer turns away wrath. I can't improve on that. Thanks, Mom.

Getting from here to there

An old story tells of the city man who was lost deep in the country. A kindly farmer attempted to give him directions. The city man, accustomed to street signs and stop lights, had trouble understanding the farmer's directions: "Follow the fence line and as the crow flies." In desperation the country gentleman said, "Well, I guess you just can't get there from here."

When anger inhibits our ability to forgive, it is hard to imagine "getting there from here." I heard a tone of pleading in the voice of a sixteen year old who said, "I just can't do it." He had a disturbing history of lashing out at others. When threats were not sufficient, he carried them out. Forgiveness had no meaning; lashing out was the only solution he had ever known. He was heading toward a youth detention center where he could be controlled.

At our first meeting, we began by reviewing times he had been mistreated. Then we did some role playing on better ways to respond. He had become particularly angry at a teacher who accused him of cheating. He reacted by pushing her and threatening to smash the windows out of her car. Suspension was the immediate result which put him in jeopardy of failing the school year.

We enacted the conflict many times before he realized he was destroying himself. Eventually, he learned he could calmly tell the teacher he was not cheating. If she refused to believe him, it would be better to forgive the injustice. At least he could increase the odds of passing the tenth grade.

A nine-year-old boy came to my office in a state of fury. When he brought home a bad report card, his mother took his television away and made him study two hours every night. Adding insult to injury, she insisted that he see me every week for the next semester.

This little guy could give sailors lessons on salty language. I allowed him to vent verbally for a few minutes before he sat down. As his temper cooled, I sat next to him—with a clipboard, pencils, and paper. This aroused his curiosity. When I determined it was safe, I gave him a pencil. Together, we wrote and drew as we discussed how he felt and how he would like to feel. An "Angryometer" began to emerge (see Figure 2).

The Angryometer is simple, but it has proved to be quite helpful. The only rule is to stay out of the "I'm confused" area. Everything above the middle is "mad, feel bad"; all below is "happy, feel good." With a crayon or marker the child fills in column A like a thermometer to identify his present feeling. He then decides how he would like to feel and fills in column B. Usually by this time, feelings are in control. With the reduction of anger, forgiveness is not so remote and becomes easier to achieve. He has gotten from here to there.

The Angryometer works equally well with teenagers and adults. One of my colleagues took it to her counseling center to use with the professional staff.

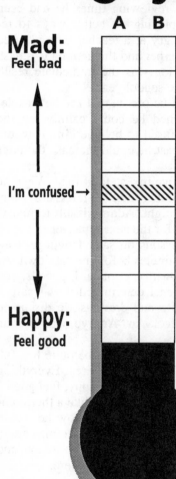

Angryometer

Mad:
Feel bad

I'm confused →

Happy:
Feel good

A   B

10-Bash brains out

9-Kick fanny

8-Cuss out

7-Say something angry

6-Make an ugly face

5-Give a smile

4-Say something pleasant

3-Give a sincere compliment

2-Share a Coke

1-Give a hug

A - How I feel
B - How I would like to feel

Figure 2

Keeping our balance

With tears in her eyes, a caring, dedicated foster mother pleaded for help. Eighteen months before, she had taken a ten-year-old boy into her home after he had been removed from his parents, a victim of beatings by his stepfather and neglect by his mother. His mother openly despised the child and used racial slurs in reference to her son and his natural father. With two children of their own, these adults had no room in their home or hearts for this intelligent child from a previous marriage.

He had been allowed to visit home twice. On the first visit he was beaten again, but fearing retaliation, did not report it. His hopes soared during his second visit when his mother told him she would petition the court for his custody. The following week they refused to accept his phone calls. A month later the family disappeared and abandoned the child to the mercy of anyone who might care for him. Eventually, authorities found the parents, but they abandoned him again.

A tireless social worker located his natural father. Again hope quickened, only to be dashed away when the man refused to see or write his son.

As his foster mother and I reviewed his tragic history, we began to understand why he was not responding despite the love and warmth he was getting in her home. He met verbal expressions of caring with sulky withdrawals. A supporting hand on his shoulder could quickly be brushed away. This experienced foster mother finally realized there would probably be no return on her emotional investment. Nevertheless, she was willing to continue to love.

Later the boy told me, "No matter what they say, I do care about them." At last he could talk about his hurt. He reasoned that the foster home would, at best, be only temporary. Fearing rejection, he had guarded his true feelings. He was, after all, only protecting himself.

When I think of this boy, I also recall a young woman his age whose circumstances were equally painful. Her mother died in surgery when she was four. Unable to function alone, her father married a domineering woman who harshly reinforced rigid discipline with an extension cord. An alert teacher reported marks on the child's legs. Attempting to avoid legal charges, the father blamed the child when the stepmother left the state. The girl was told she had caused the family to break up.

A succession of shelters and foster homes followed. Her father would not allow her to return home. Multiple placements were necessary because of her intense emotional displays. Her temper tantrums were extreme and there was no reasoning with this youngster; she was angry—lashing out at the world.

On the surface, these two children seemed very different. His reactions were implosive; hers, explosive. However, both expressed similar hurts and rage. Both were restricted in emotional and social development and had been knocked out of balance. They were becoming dysfunctional, unforgiving, bitter adults.

Understanding children helps to understand adults. Like these two preteens, adults, too, get out of balance and fail to resolve the conflicts in their turbulent lives. They may never learn forgiveness.

Keeping emotional and rational balance is vital to effective forgiveness (Figure 3B). Some, like the young woman, fail to forgive because they are focused on their emotions. They do not understand that they alone are suffering from their own hostility (Figure 3A). Others, like the young man, fail to forgive because they cannot allow themselves to experience inner pain. They feel no need to forgive (Figure 3C).

Occasionally, hyperemotional people (Figure 3A) marry hyperrational partners (Figure 3B) in an attempt to achieve balance. This is a sure course for disaster. Neither possesses forgiveness skills so they usually end up in either hot or cold war. Balance is an individual task. Two balanced people have a chance.

Balance is a step toward forgiveness. It helps to avoid extremes in feelings and behavior which inhibit personal growth and social adjustment. Extremes found among institutionalized child victims of abuse illustrate well the need for balance. Some become so emotionally detached they neither feel nor talk about their emotions. They easily live without friends. Others let their own emotional deficits enslave them and they become emotionally dependent or sexually promiscuous in an attempt to fill the void. Many make adjustments simply by becoming miniature grown-ups and, at times, they may try to help others. Adult attempts at achieving balance are really no different.

Achieving balance and maintaining it takes practice. Actually, without realizing it, we can adjust rational/emotional balance at will. The more we practice this self-imposed discipline, the easier it becomes.

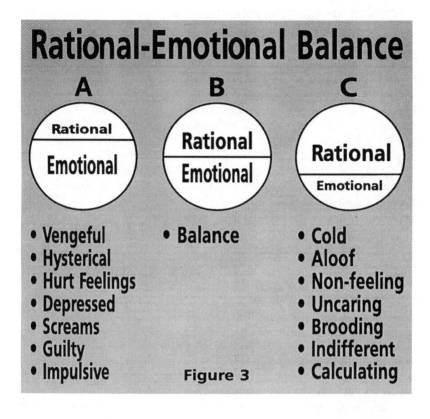

Rational-Emotional Balance

A

Rational

Emotional

- Vengeful
- Hysterical
- Hurt Feelings
- Depressed
- Screams
- Guilty
- Impulsive

B

Rational

Emotional

- Balance

Figure 3

C

Rational

Emotional

- Cold
- Aloof
- Non-feeling
- Uncaring
- Brooding
- Indifferent
- Calculating

Because hyperemotional people thrive on excitement, balance threatens to make life seem boring. Why experience the tranquility of reading a book when there is stimulating violence and hostility on television? Better yet, real violence in the home with real blood keeps life from ever getting dull.

Hyperrational people may also be reluctant to achieve balance. Rationalizing, intellectualizing, or minimizing problems are relatively painless. People who are overly rational are not very exciting, but they are always cool.

Balance allows people to feel and deal with pain. Balance helps us forgive, and forgiveness helps maintain balance.

Choosing the right nervous system

While talking with a distraught mother of five, I asked if she had a history of emotional problems. She replied, "No, but I've had three nervous breakdowns." Most of us can identify with her. The term "nervous breakdown" is not in the official nomenclature of psychiatric disorders, but the feeling is nearly universal. The image of shattered nerves is not only descriptive, it's also familiar. It means losing control.

Police picked up a thirteen-year-old boy for truancy. The youth also had a long history of fighting and vandalism. Standing before the court, the boy went out of control and threw a chair at the judge. Considerable destruction took place before authorities could restrain him. Because he was out of control, he was sent to a state facility. Sadly, he forfeited his own right to control himself.

"I can't do it," means "I won't do it" or "I'm out of control." Most people who make statements such as these believe what they are saying. They see no way out. Anger controls them from within.

Fortunately, self-control is not as remote as we might believe. Physiologically, the body has two nervous systems. The central nervous system controls voluntary movement; the autonomic nervous system governs involuntary movement or function. Holding up three fingers on the right hand is accomplished through the central nervous system. Heartbeat is regulated by the autonomic. Both systems regulate some functions such as breathing or eye blinking which can be voluntary and involuntary.

When anger goes out of control, we turn it over to the autonomic system. However, to scream, throw things, or carry out premeditated revenge requires use of the central nervous system and is strictly at our command. "I can't help it" is not a valid excuse unless there is some type of neurologic disease or lesion. In that case, we might have to be permanently restrained for our own protection and the protection of others.

Human beings can choose which nervous system to use to express anger. The choice puts us back in control. But with control comes responsibility.

The autonomic system tends to react. Action is taken without thought. The central system has the capacity to respond. Action is taken after thought or deliberation. The brain is the executive that decides the system. We can control brain decisions even in the heat of anger.

An angry wife complained that she could not help screaming at her husband. I suggested that she could, indeed, help it. As she took a deep breath to prepare for one of her tirades for my benefit, I asked her to close her mouth and breathe only through her nose. When she did this, she regained control. My request was actually an exercise for employing the central nervous system. Later, she learned she could control what she said, the tones she used, and the most effective decibel level. She soon outgrew her need for a marriage counselor.

A young factory worker found extreme difficulty restraining his anger toward his estranged wife and her family. He felt she had chosen her mother over him. She had left, taking everything, including his shorts. He feared he might go out of control. Together we searched for control mechanisms. Finally, he decided not to talk to her for a week. His attorney would channel all communication. After all, he reasoned, he was paying his lawyer to "take the heat for him." A good central nervous system decision; anger came under control.

Anger control can have a profound effect on relationships. Six months after her wedding, a lovely young bride in tears sat in my office. Her dreams had turned to nightmares. As we discussed the problem, it became evident that she had grown up in a home where emotional displays were common. Anger was expressed in wild dramatic scenes or went unrecognized. Each scene superseded the last brouhaha. This habit quickly put her marriage in jeopardy.

Happily, she realized she could express love with little or no difficulty. She had good communication skills. Balance meant that she use her rational skills to control expressions of anger. In therapy, we role-played her first attempts to respond rather than react. Soon she took her refined skills home and saved her marriage.

Imbalance is a major obstacle to forgiveness. However, once we are back in balance, we tame the anger and forgiveness doesn't seem too formidable.

GETTING OVER THE MOUNTAIN
"Hey, maybe this is possible after all."

Time for action

I recall a bittersweet conversation with a woman who said she felt much better after she forgave her father for his inability to express love. "I never heard him say, 'I love you' to anyone," she recalled. "I hated him for being so cold."

But now life was different. She was able to forgive her father and freely gave and accepted love in her own family. She vowed that each day she would assure her children of her love for them. But with a note of longing sadness, she said softly, "I only wish I had forgiven him before his last stroke. We never knew if he was aware of anything after that. It might have meant something to him. I wish I knew."

Once we have clarified the cause and intensity of our feelings and have gained control over our anger, forgiveness becomes a realistic goal. However, climbing to the summit does not mean we have to go over the mountain. The trip to the bottom is easier than the climb so far and is perhaps easier than getting over the top. The choice is always ours; delay, nevertheless, can be costly. The time for action has arrived. There will be opportunities for refinement in the future.

From his own observation, Dr. Glenn Doman maintains that a mental process seems to take place in children at about age six. After that age, learning capacity is greatly restructured. For instance, the likelihood of learning a second language is significantly reduced. Prior to this time, children in the right environment can learn several languages at the same time.[3]

This is true of forgiveness. Adults do not forgive as easily as children. An emotional malignancy may seem in remission. In reality the disease goes on. Unforgiveness does not take a holiday. It becomes increasingly more difficult to identify the causes of bitterness and to heal from the savage wounds that our own animosity has inflicted on us.

Nothing happens until we make it happen. Delay accomplishes nothing. Robert Ackerman expressed it well in his book, *Let Go and Grow*.[4]

Some of us grew up on old sayings such as "Fish or cut bait" or "Take the bull by the horns." A widely quoted political figure was more emphatic but less delicate when he said, "It's time to shit or get off the pot."

Marking a specific time can be helpful in our commitment to accomplish forgiveness. For instance, writing a detailed account of our anger and burning it with a ritual may affirm our determination to get better. Other rituals might include prayer, meditation, or private cathartic raging. Such ceremonies may be traditional or uniquely personal. They are not magic but they mark symbolically that point when forgiveness was born.

Definitive action can lead to success, but success can be frightening. A thirty-two-year-old woman was able eventually to forgive her ex-husband when he attempted to avoid child support by charging her with abusing their son. Authorities took the child away from her. When the truth finally became known, she was granted custody of the boy, but her life was shattered. She had never succeeded at anything. Having had only a limited education, she had never held a steady job. The idea of placing the child in foster care was tempting; her fear of having to succeed as a single mother was nearly overwhelming.

Nevertheless, she did not give up easily. Her love for her son inspired in her a new confidence heretofore unknown. By working at any honest job she could find and sharing parental supervision duties with other single mothers, she eventually worked her way toward a degree in business accounting. But panic struck. Unconsciously, she began to self-destruct. School attendance dropped, grades fell, sleepless nights haunted her.

Fortunately, we uncovered the source of her fear. She had never known success. She knew how to fail, but she was lost in a world populated by successful people. At this point, she made an irrevocable commitment to succeed. She climbed over the mountain and became a successful mother with a promising career.

Forgiveness is frightening in the same way. We know how to be bitter and hateful. Life on the other side of the mountain may be unknown territory. An irrevocable commitment to forgive can put us over the top. No, we do not become perfect. We may have worlds yet to forgive but at last we know a better way is possible.

Some of us become addicted to our own bitterness. We do not know how to live without it. As with any other addiction, we must call an abrupt halt to the destructive behavior and not allow it to recur. Forgiveness is the avenue to recovery—one day at a time.

The most common temptation is to put the need to forgive on hold. Excuses abound but decisive action ends the delay that perpetuates the hurt. Healing begins when forgiveness takes place.

Naomi a.k.a. Mara

The case of Naomi, also known as Mara, may be one of the most vivid descriptions ever recorded of the contrast between bitterness and betterness. Naomi's experiences, found in the biblical Book of Ruth, could prove helpful when we feel defeated.

Drought forced Naomi and her husband to leave their farm and move to Moab. They found it difficult to leave their home and relocate in a foreign country. For Naomi, tragedy did not stop there. Her husband and both of her married sons died, leaving three destitute widows.

Determined to survive, Naomi and her daughter-in-law, Ruth, returned to their old home near Bethlehem. As Naomi and Ruth approached the city, friends gathered to greet them. They called out "Naomi" (meaning pleasant). She spewed out her frustration and insisted they call her "Mara" (meaning bitter). Her bitterness was so pervasive that it became a part of her identity.

The depth of her agony and eventual recovery has inspired many for centuries. She discovered the road to healing and shared it in her story. She found spiritual resources beyond herself.

Sometimes our bitterness gets so great that we cannot overcome it alone. We must look beyond ourselves for help. This does not imply that we look to a greater Power to do it for us. It is more productive to use that Power to do it for ourselves. I used to pray, "Lord, open doors for me." I have abandoned that prayer for a more meaningful one: "Lord, give me the strength to open doors for myself."

Spiritual resources transcend religious beliefs or affiliations. Many find strength in organized religions while others find it in nature or personal experiences that affirm the power of love. Spirituality is a force in everyone's life. It enables us to reach beyond human limitations. I learned a lesson in humility when I realized that people with radically different beliefs are often much better people than I. For example, Mahatma Ghandi's culture and faith are strange to me, yet his ability to love and forgive had an impact on the world. Fortunately, one does not have to adhere to the "right religion" to draw from spiritual reserves.

Forgiveness is not indicative of moral or spiritual superiority. It is merely a means toward good emotional and spiritual health.

The value of spiritual guidance was obvious in the life of a woman who came to me in a state of severe physical and emotional pain. Few people become so bitter or suffer so much. Within a year her husband died and she underwent three surgical procedures on her spine. The pain was almost unbearable. She became bitter and alienated from her family who were so involved in dividing her husband's estate that they showed little concern for her. Friends and neighbors attempted to call on her, but she resisted their efforts. Consequently, she found herself alone. Physical and emotional pain were her only companions.

Our first session was a disaster. Neither of us liked the other. This impasse lasted a few weeks as we tolerated each other. We had little hope for improvement until, quite suddenly, she was like a new person in the same body. Her face radiated with life, her voice was calm and kind. Moreover, her physical pain was greatly reduced. She spent most of an entire session telling me how she had found spiritual strength quietly in the privacy of her home. Forgiveness had been a spiritual experience. As she left, she thanked me profusely for my help. Although I appreciated her graciousness, I reminded her that I could not take credit for her transformation. She remained in therapy for several months but I gained as much—even more—from it than she did.

Spirituality is personal, but others can offer spiritual guidance. Perfect people do not exist, but many wonderful imperfect people can be helpful. Clergy, therapists, and friends are common sources. Counselees should not expect them to reinforce bitterness but give help to look beyond ourselves and tap into the Power that has created and sustained the universe. No doubt Ruth was such a friend for Naomi:

> "Entreat me not to leave you or return from following you; for where you go I will go, and where you lodge I will lodge; your people will be my people, and your God my God; where you die I will die, and there will I be buried ...."[5]

One step at a time

Learning to forgive is much like learning to fall in love. There are no precise procedures, but guidelines may be helpful. If we want love, it helps to act lovely. To stop being bitter, it helps to act better.

Guidelines are helpful. Full elaboration on these is unnecessary here since the concepts are discussed elsewhere. Just a capsulization may be beneficial (see Figure 4).

Recognition of misery. A personal inventory assessing hurt and damage clarifies bitterness.

Motivation to change. As a rule, we can do what we want to do. We achieve sufficient motivation when our desire to get better overcomes our wish to stay bitter.

Commitment to action. Ideas, concepts, hopes, and forgiveness mean nothing until we invest energy, setting them into motion. They are only mental images until they come alive in us.

Rational understanding. To understand the reason someone has hurt us is not a prerequisite to forgiveness; nevertheless, it does help.

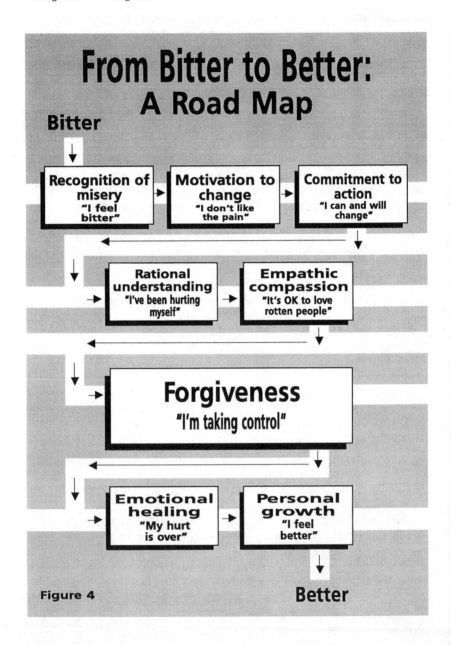

From Bitter to Better:
A Road Map

Bitter

| Recognition of misery "I feel bitter" | → | Motivation to change "I don't like the pain" | → | Commitment to action "I can and will change" |

| Rational understanding "I've been hurting myself" | → | Empathic compassion "It's OK to love rotten people" |

Forgiveness
"I'm taking control"

| Emotional healing "My hurt is over" | → | Personal growth "I feel better" |

Better

Figure 4

94

Understanding alone can intensify bitterness, but it is also the means to gain insight into human behavior.

Empathic compassion. Neither understanding nor compassion is based on approving the behavior of an offender. We accomplish empathy best when we separate the person from his or her outrageous conduct.

Forgiveness. Forgiveness is not something we do for others. On the contrary, we do it for ourselves. The one forgiven may not know or even care, but it is rewarding when they do.

Emotional healing. Forgiveness cleanses emotional wounds; it is a balm that heals. The soreness does not indicate a failure to forgive. Healing takes time.

Personal growth. Forgiveness and emotional healing foster personal growth. This does not eliminate the possibility of being hurt again. It is merely a lesson that teaches an important skill.

A list of procedural steps can be misleading. Realistically, a few setbacks and some major falls may impede progress. This results in one step forward and two steps back. When this happens, forgive yourself; remember how much "better" feels than "bitter."

Use the old brain stem

It takes more than one heroic episode to become a forgiving person. Each episode is a step in the right direction. Feeling better is the outgrowth of forgiveness. Sustained emotional and physical health comes when we incorporate this forgiveness into our personalities.

A function of the brain stem is to take over repetitive tasks. For example, most of us remember learning to ride a bicycle. Those first efforts were awkward and usually ended in a fall. To master the skill, we learned a number of psychomotor operations which soon became natural. Pedaling, for instance, was a conscious left foot, right foot, left foot, right foot process until it became automatic. Eventually, we would pedal for miles without conscious thought. The brain stem took over the function. We will likely retain that skill for the rest of our lives.

To live as a forgiving person requires practice and energy. This is true also for being hateful and bitter. The difference? Forgiveness is constructive and builds strength. Bitterness, on the other hand, is an emotional disease which weakens.

Forgiveness requires considerable practice from day to day with a strong likelihood that mortals will never develop it to perfection. Better luck in the next world, but practice in this life is worth the effort.

Forgiveness does not come naturally any more than riding a bicycle, reading, or tying shoes. Forgiveness is an acquired skill. Like other developed skills, we have the option of not using them. But who wants to be illiterate or go through life with their shoes untied.

To practice forgiveness until it becomes a brain stem function is a worthy challenge. Like learning to ride a bicycle, we may feel clumsy and frustrated. Crashes are inevitable. But patience pays dividends. Because old habits die hard, we must permit ourselves to feel awkward as we overcome them. It is helpful to tell supportive friends that we are trying to learn new skills. Eventually, old habits will fade and new ones will emerge.

Old habits are more easily broken if new ones replace them. As an example, many parents are extremely critical of their children. Most of these parents were raised on heavy diets of carping with generous amounts of caviling for dessert. I meet them when they seek help for their children who have, somehow, lost their self-esteem.

I recall a mother who sat for two hours telling me all that was wrong with her small sons. I quickly sensed what was happening and sent the boys to the waiting room to protect them from this onslaught of criticism. Two hours did not give her enough time to ventilate, but I managed to help her recognize at least one good thing about each son. In later sessions, I disallowed negative statements about the boys. She gradually learned to identify their good qualities and to give them the approval they so desperately needed. Her first efforts were weak, but with time they became stronger. The boys improved beyond all expectations. Finally, she realized that therapy had done nothing directly for the youngsters. The major changes came about when she developed new habits.

At one time I lived near a place where the old Santa Fe Trail was still visible. An endless train of wagons had cut ruts in the rock which could still be seen. Other locations along the trail with less rock were cut deeper. Eventually, the ruts in some places became so deep the trail had to be moved a few feet and new ruts started. Great care had to be taken to keep the wagons from slipping into the old ruts and getting mired down.

The brain stem allows new ruts to begin, but with practice, forgiveness becomes more natural. One must take care to avoid the old ruts; they are deep and treacherous. Eventually, new ruts guide us toward becoming better, more forgiving people.

CHAPTER V

Forgiving, Healing, and Growing

For several years I have been a member of a multidisciplinary team which holds professional workshops to help communities utilize their resources for abused children and their families. At the end of a hard day's work, we conclude with a segment called "So what, now what, where do we go from here?" The objective is to dialogue with community leaders to insure the growth and development of services to victimized youngsters.

The question, "So what, now what, where do we go from here?" is particularly relevant at this time. You and I have explored resisting forgiveness, recognizing the need to forgive, beginning with self-forgiveness, and becoming a forgiving person. Each of these represents important milestones toward becoming a better person. The task now is to stay better and to continue to grow.

The quest for improvement is consistent with human history. In addition to basic taboos, modern life is built on an evolution of numerous social rules. Personal hygiene would have meant very little to our more primitive ancestors. Bad breath, body odor, and dandruff were not vital issues. Even toilet paper was not introduced until the 1880s.[1]

Today's modern populace enjoys improved health and quality of life through these and other social customs. We have achieved these improvements largely by building onto basic social laws that have stood the test of time and have proved to be essential to civilized living—the value of human life, for instance.

Forgiveness is a time-honored law which provides a foundation for emotional, spiritual, and social stability. We attain healing and growth by building onto forgiveness. This is no less important to our total development than soap, toothpaste, and toilet paper.

Forgiving, healing, and growing form a triadic partnership essential to personal maturity or a better way of life. The sequence of these three is important. Forgiveness sterilizes the wound, permits healing, and, in turn, generates growth. Maxwell Maltz, a plastic surgeon, describes the process in terms of facial surgery:

> In facial surgery there can be no partial, tentative, or halfway measures. The scar tissue is cut out, completely and entirely. The wound is allowed to heal cleanly. And care is taken to see that the face will be restored in every particular, just as it was before injury and just as if the injury had never been.[2]

People often resist therapy by asserting, "I'm not crazy!" I usually respond by asking, "But are you happy?" To be unable or unwilling to forgive is not necessarily "crazy" but it certainly leads to unhappiness.

Maintaining a mature lifestyle is a continuing process. Attitude, compassion, and understanding demand constant fine-tuning, even complete periodic overhauls.

Better is not perfect. But by becoming better, the challenge assures ongoing health and growth. Forgiving one major hurt is not an assurance that other offenses are forgiven nor that new hurts won't keep coming. However, the skill to forgive and recover will contribute to ongoing personal development. There is no end to forgiving, healing, and growing. That is exciting!

This final chapter covers a few pitfalls, problems, and goals in view of forgiveness, healing, and growth. "When forgiveness fails" is a feeling we all experience. "Forgiving the unforgivable" is perhaps one of life's most rigorous emotional and spiritual exercises. Aspiring to the major leagues provides an opportunity to determine where we are and where we would like to go.

WHEN FORGIVENESS FAILS
"I knew it all along."

The perpetual perpetrator

Now and then anxiety over an offense will not go away, and we are helpless to change the situation. One man, extremely frustrated by his boss, said, "It's hard to forgive some son of a bitch who will always be a son of a bitch."

My young friends frequently complain of similar frustrations. Some children seem to take delight in torturing other children. Cruel name-calling and physical hazing are not uncommon. They feel helpless and angry; they don't understand why bullies seek them out for mistreatment.

When this happens, I attempt to help children distinguish the difference between "pickees" and "pickors." Pickees are on the receiving end of the pickor's misbehavior. Pickees are usually sensitive emotionally, but they have no insight into the sadistic pleasure pickors gain through cruelty. Pickors seek out pickees since it guarantees an emotional upheaval. The same phenomenon takes place in flocks of chickens. Pickors peck pickees until the pickees die from the abuse. Among children, pickees sometime grow up and become serious pickors, inflicting violent crimes on other people. Others remain lifelong victims.

Pickors are people who feel inferior but who get their jollies running over others, hoping to overcome their feelings of inadequacy. Once pickees learn to avoid becoming upset, they no longer reinforce the sick needs of pickors, and the cycle is broken. Pickees find new courage when they abandon their unwittingly masochistic interactions with sadistic pickors. As forgiveness comes easier, pickees get stronger and pickors seem less intimidating.

Uncomfortable instinctive reactions toward someone who perpetually hurts us is natural and does not necessarily indicate that we have failed to forgive. Those wrenching gut feelings may be normal "fight or flight" responses. Keep in mind, healing may take a lot longer than forgiving. This is especially true when someone who seems to have a vested interest in our agony or humiliation confronts us.

We may find it difficult to forgive persons we cannot trust, respect, or love. Perpetual perpetrators fall into this category. Fortunately, to forgive does not demand trust, respect, or love. Of course, we should feel Christian or universal love toward everyone, but we do not have to live with or allow ourselves to be subjected to their abusive behavior.

Love and trust are often confused. Some time ago I talked with some parents who were having serious problems with their seventeen-year-old daughter. She had been arrested three times for driving the family car under the influence of alcohol and drugs. The parents were very angry. When I asked why they had not taken her car privileges away, the father explained, "We can't do that; we love her." I went on to question whether or not they trusted their daughter. After all, her behavior was less than trustworthy. I certainly would not have trusted her with my car. Once these parents understood they could love their daughter without trusting her, they forgave her but took firm action to halt her irresponsible behavior. The young woman was, of course, upset but her parents felt much better.

Perpetual perpetrators usually do not care how much suffering they heap upon others. It is absurd to trust and respect these people. We build trust and respect. Perpetual perpetrators destroy. They are not worth suffering emotional malignancies.

How long or how many times should we forgive? Is seventy times seven enough? Should we keep score so that after the 145th offense we can finally kick ass? The real question is, how much forgiveness do we need to give to get better and stay that way? Indeed, forgiveness is very personal.

The right to hate

Forgiveness often fails because we refuse to forfeit the right to hate. No one can argue that severely victimized children have a right to hate. Many get much social support for hating those who have selfishly dumped tragedy into their young lives. Rights are hard to relinquish.

My young friends are often curious about my habit of riding a motorcycle. When we talk about giving up the right to hate, I ask them to imagine riding down a busy street with me. As we approach an intersection we pretend to have a green light but notice that an eight-wheel transport truck is speeding into the intersection against a red light. "What should I do?" I ask. Of course they tell me to stop. I remind them that I have the green light and, therefore, have a right to go through the intersection. To stop would mean giving up my right. Yet, to insist on my right would spell sure death for both of us. One little boy said, "I'd jump off and let that truck mash you flat." The need to turn loose of hate and forgive becomes obvious.

Hatred is legal. No one can wrest from us this right to hate. Nicotine and alcohol are also legal and we have a right to use them. But our best interest is not always served by insisting on our rights.

Hate campaigns can generate a lot of social support. This is especially true when hatred is considered a right worth dying for. In extreme cases, hate evolves into war and people die.

Pedophiles—those who have sexual preference for children—are almost universally scorned and hated. Even in prison they are treated with contempt and subjected to beatings by hardened criminals. Compassion and forgiveness for these people may be hard to imagine, especially if you or your child have been victimized. As a victim, you indeed have the right to hate.

To forgive and give up the right to hate pedophiles does not mean they should be free. They are dangerous people, threatening the emotional and physical well-being of children. Sometimes they murder to cover up their crimes. They do not generally respond to psychotherapy and many must be kept in prison to protect children.

But imagine the torment a pedophile must experience. Some prefer incarceration, fearing their own impulses. One cannot hate him as much as he hates himself. The right to hate only fires hell inside ourselves. His fires could be no more hideous.

Forgiveness requires giving up our right to hate. It also helps us channel our energy toward productive rights. For instance, the "right to life, liberty, and the pursuit of happiness" can be lost by insisting on our right to hate. The right to forgive, love, and exercise compassion is much more productive, assuring healing and growth.

Growth is not always pleasant

At times, forgiveness fails because we do not want to grow up. While we have no control over our chronological age—Ponce de Leon didn't find the fountain of youth, but he certainly deserves an "A" for effort—we can control our emotional and spiritual maturity.

An elderly grandmother complained that she had been the sole support for her three grandchildren since the day they were born. Her daughter, mother of the children, was in her thirties and seldom showed any interest in them. She was free to drink, use drugs, and live with a succession of men. Growing up and accepting mature responsibility would put an end to her party life. As long as this grandmother continued to underwrite her lifestyle, the mother would not change. After all, responsibility is not fun.

Personal healing and growth involve lifting ourselves and others. Forgiveness makes this possible. We become responsible for developing compassion toward ourselves and others. Lifting up is always harder than pushing down. Growing up is hard.

Teenagers think they want to grow up until they are faced with adult responsibility. This is not unique to adolescents. Consider the maturity we need to develop empathy for those who hurt us.

Empathy can be a point of human contact with someone we presently hate. It somehow acknowledges that the offender has worth as a human being. It is much easier to classify the person as scum bag than to forgive, heal, and grow.

Attitude is another difficult area of growth. A forgiving attitude may be hard to achieve and even harder to maintain, but the rewards are rich and fulfilling. Fortunately, when we are motivated, attitude becomes more easily controlled.

Attitude has at least three components so interlaced that to change one heavily influences the other two (Figure 5). These components include thinking, feeling, and behaving. As the three tend to be harmonious with one another, discord in one area creates sour notes in the other two. Conversely, positive change of one component will promote beneficial changes in the other two. Attitude is back in balance.

To change attitude effectively, it is helpful to consider the components that we can most easily change. Once that change is made, the other two will fall into harmony with a little encouragement.

The choice of component is a personal decision and may vary with individual personality, time, and situation. For example, we may have a low opinion (thinking) and contempt (feeling) for the offender and still treat the person with dignity (behavior). By controlling our behavior, we are better equipped to reshape our thinking and modify our feelings. Thus, the result is a more forgiving and mature attitude.

On another occasion we may consider the perpetrator to be selfish (thinking) and lash out at his selfishness (behavior), but find compassion (feeling) for his selfishness. Allowing feelings of compassion to modify our thinking and behavior puts our attitude back into balance.

Anger, hate, and hostility are feelings that easily trigger retaliatory behaviors. These feelings may be the most common form of attitude dysfunction. In this situation, thinking is the most likely candidate for change. With some clear thinking, it becomes obvious that our feelings and behaviors are self-destructive and have no impact on the person who has wronged us. Once again attitude comes back into balance. Forgiveness is more easily achieved.

Growing up had been hard for a teenage friend. One day he came bounding into my office, waving a piece of paper in his hand. He had

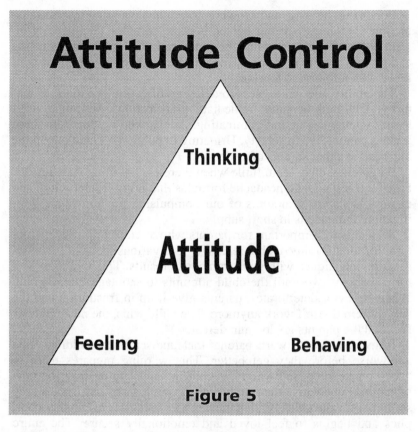

Attitude Control

Thinking

Attitude

Feeling

Behaving

Figure 5

earned his driver's license, an important rite of passage in our society. Life would never be the same. He felt new power and a heady sense of personal independence. He had reached a major milestone and had reason to celebrate.

Forgiveness is a similar rite of passage. It opens up new power and independence through healing and growth. Growth is not always pleasant but forgiveness is a milestone worthy of celebration.

Giving up too soon

Attempting to reduce stress in his life, an overworked business manager came up with a new motto: "If at first you don't succeed, to hell with it!" Most of us can identify with his feeling.

Forgiving, healing, and growing do not always bring instant satisfaction. Becoming a better person is more complex than making instant coffee. Forgiveness may be more rapid but subsequent healing and growth require more time. Incomplete healing should not be confused with a failure to forgive.

The ability and willingness to delay gratification is a mark of maturity. Children demand immediate gratification. An infant must learn to delay eating and eliminating. Adults who do not learn these lessons cannot live in society. Urinating in public will land one in the same jail as other serious offenders.

Forgiveness may seem futile when there are not immediate results. Fast-food restaurants, headache formulas that bring instant relief, and express lanes are symptoms of our compulsion for immediate gratification. Patience is in short supply.

Persistence is important for parents who attempt to provide structure for undisciplined children. We use various behavioral modification techniques with good immediate results. This might go well for a week or two until the child attempts to sabotage the program. When behavior deteriorates, parents give it up in frustration and the new system doesn't work anymore. The child wins, the new methods fail, and the parents go down in defeat.

I have learned to warn parents that undisciplined children often get worse before they get better. This warning prepares them to "keep on keeping on" when the child attempts to destroy the new structure. I encourage them to be consistent, loving, and firm as they set limits for the child. With patience, the youngster eventually complies and begins to feel loved and emotionally secure. The entire family gets better.

The process of forgiving and getting better is not easy, often encumbered with setbacks. Bitter thoughts and feelings and the desire to retaliate have a way of creeping back into old dominant positions. We may even welcome them. When growth is not pleasant and we feel defeated, the bitterness may feel good and be particularly tempting. Fortunately, setbacks are not defeats. A lost battle does not mean the war is lost.

An alcoholic, in recovery for over ten years, suffered the loss of his wife. She died suddenly about the same time he was fired and cheated out of his retirement. Bitter and alone, he sought out his old "friend." However, he came quickly for help and with patience forgave himself and others. He began to heal and grow once again.

Giving up too soon is easy; patience is more difficult. By being patient with the toxic effects of chronic hostility, we allow bitterness to poison our lives for many years. In all personal fairness we should give patience toward getting better equal time. Forty years of bitterness should be worth forty years of betterness. Giving up at all is giving up too soon.

FORGIVING THE UNFORGIVABLE
"Sure! And horses have wings."

How far is far enough?

One of my first encounters as a young student was with a seriously disturbed man who believed he had committed the unpardonable sin. He was a good person but he lived in a state of never-ending self-condemnation. Seldom have I seen anyone suffer such excruciating emotional pain. Forgiveness for him was always just out of reach.

What is forgivable and what is not forgivable is an inevitable question—and a reasonable one, but in the wrong direction. The real question asks what are we willing or not willing to forgive.

Without exception, every lecture I give on psychotherapeutic forgiveness includes someone who poses a situation that seems unforgivable such as murder, rape, abuse, and mayhem. Yet the question remains: how far are we willing to go to forgive?

Only we can set those limits. Nothing is unforgivable unless we make it so. However, unwillingness to forgive major crimes inflicted on us is understandable. Hatred may win the support of friends or even society at large, but the emotional disease is locked inside and the damage continues. No rules declare that we cannot go beyond human limitations. Our commitment to forgive, then, should be no less limited.

Victims of Acquired Immune Deficiency Syndrome (AIDS) are confronted with the challenge of forgiving the unforgivable. For many, the choice is to die in bitterness or to die with self-respect. A willingness to forgive can put meaning into life and enables one to die with dignity.

Victims of AIDS usually lose dignity and find themselves associated with societal perceptions of sexual perversion, drug addiction, moral degeneration, and loneliness. Their suicide rate is sixty-six times more frequent than in the general population.[3] They often prefer death rather than live with their shame.

Forgiveness for AIDS patients is complex and serves as a model for developing insight into major issues that call for forgiveness. Self-forgiveness is crucial. Forgiving oneself for sexual indiscretions, vulnerability, or transmitting the disease to the unborn is vital.

Victims must also forgive society for its uncharitable attitude toward the disease. Even innocent children, victims of the disease, have known isolation and rejection to the extent that some communities barred them from friends and school.

However the disease is contracted, the victim must wrestle with the need to forgive at least one other person. The virus had another host.

Any terminal disease forces us to face philosophical or theological questions. Some burn with anger at God and perceive death as a punishment. Others battle with themselves in a spiritual conflict. They look to God for hope and peace but are furious that God would allow such a cruel suffering and death.

A soldier dies with dignity and becomes a hero. An AIDS victim also dies and in forgiving the unforgivable he restores dignity; this is truly heroic.

Internal bitterness is an emotional carcinogen and only forgiveness eradicates it. It makes little difference whether the offense is forgivable or unforgivable. The internal damage is the same.

How far is far enough? It is far enough when we are finally able to forgive, heal, and grow.

Breaking down barriers

A few years ago some scientists considered the "sound barrier" as the ultimate speed humans could attain. "Mach I" was soon superceded by "Mach II"—twice the speed of sound. Modern scientists tell us space travel will not be realistic until we approach the light barrier.

Many perceive the "unforgivable" as the ultimate barrier. This, of course, is not a precise scientific barrier. What I perceive as unforgivable may be elementary for you. Barriers are personal; they may change from time to time and from one situation to another within the same individual. Barriers are self-imposed, but they effectively block forgiveness, healing, and growth.

Just as Sherlock Holmes had his Moriarity, most of us have encountered at least one such nemesis—Greek for "pain in the ass." I have had several. At one time, I was steeped in rage about the attacks of a particular individual who layered one hurt over another. Forgiveness seemed impossible until a personal tragedy struck him and he turned to me for help. My first impulse was to tell him to go to hell. I entertained thoughts of gleefully watching him squirm. Instead, I gave him the help he needed and, ironically, helped myself far more than I helped him. I learned that the unforgivable is forgivable. I felt better.

Successful people generally follow four basic rules to achieve: set goals, identify barriers, overcome barriers, actualize goals. A casual observation of successful people can indicate that barriers for some are challenges for others. Successful people do not waste time blaming circumstances or other persons. They channel their energy into overcoming whatever barriers inhibit their achievement.

When I once asked a successful entrepreneur if he feared going broke, he quickly replied, "I have already lost three fortunes; I can always make another." Not only had he learned to overcome barriers, but he also learned to keep old barriers down and to overcome new ones.

The human barrier is often cited as standing in the way of forgiving the unforgivable. "I'm only human," is a legitimate plea. The world needs more saints, but most of us do not qualify for sainthood. Forgiving the unforgivable may be commonplace for saints but it remains one of life's most persistent challenges for most of us. Nevertheless, we can do a few saintly things starting with forgiveness and compassion.

Compassion can shatter a barrier since it allows for human weaknesses in ourselves and others. Recognizing shared human nature enables us to reach offenders empathetically. If forgiveness has meaning for us, it is likely to have meaning for the offender. Compassion helps to motivate forgiveness. When we hurt someone, we hope that person can forgive us. Likewise, those who hurt us would want our forgiveness. Compassion facilitates that forgiveness.

Compassion is also appropriate for those who inflict pain on us but show no remorse for their action. When we realize how emotionally impoverished uncaring people are, we break an interior barrier. Compassion is strengthened by asking ourselves if we would trade places with such heartless individuals.

Fire-breathing dragons

Not all dragons are extinct nor do they hide, tucked safely away in mythical caves. There are real dragons more dangerous than any ferocious, fire-breathing breed. There are also modern-day dragon slayers.

Live dragons are not cruel people who commit unforgivable crimes. Rather, they are those monsters of bitterness that live parasitically in our souls. Brave men and women who venture into their own deep recesses and courageously forgive even the unforgivable are today's dragon slayers.

We commit no offense in attempting to forgive rotten people. Some authorities maintain that there are individuals who can never be salvaged or rehabilitated. A few prisons are no longer correctional institutions. Instead, they serve primarily as penal institutions designed to punish. They warehouse incorrigibles to protect society.

Forgiving those who commit heinous crimes does not suggest that the perpetrators be released from prison. With forgiveness, we attempt to slay the dragons of rage that breathe fire within us. It does not arbitrarily mean reconciliation. Forgiveness and reconciliation are not the same. Reconciliation may not be feasible.

A serial murderer was put to death in Florida's electric chair. On the day of his execution, a crowd gathered outside the prison walls proclaiming the day as "fry-day." A cheer went up when he died. Some celebrated as his body was taken away. Others complained bitterly that the murderer had had the opportunity to repent and make peace with his Maker—an option he had not given his victims.

The crowd's feelings were monstrous but not abnormal. Such feelings give evidence of inner dragons—still very much alive. Those who commit hideous crimes do not deserve forgiveness, but that can be said of any offender. If forgiveness were deserved, it would not be necessary and fire-breathing dragons would become an endangered species.

Rescue from relapse

Betterness is not a perpetual state of happiness. Good health requires care, maintenance, and occasional intervention. This is especially true when we are confronted with forgiving major unforgivable injuries. We can easily forgive small hurts that soon heal.

Major offenses are not so easy. Hurts once forgiven can be resuscitated and we are in agony again. Hatred, bitterness, and revenge have a way of returning, and we wonder if forgiveness is really possible.

Relapses, not necessarily preventable, are always forgivable. Visceral reactions may occur and keep hate alive or warn of impending relapse.

Unwanted symptoms have a purpose. Pain calls attention to an injured part of the body. Fever helps the body fight infection. Nevertheless, pain and fever can be debilitating. Pain can render the whole organism useless; fever can damage the brain permanently. Symptoms must be taken seriously and treated.

So it is with bitterness. The earlier symptoms are detected, the easier they are to treat. When a person perceives hurt as unforgivable, the potential for internal harm is astronomical.

In a similar way, it is important to develop an immunity to the toxicity of the unforgivable. Forgiving when forgiveness seems impossible is healing and strengthening in itself. This level of forgiveness is a major step toward getting better and staying that way.

ASPIRING TO THE MAJOR LEAGUES
"Nobody bats a thousand."

Nonforgiveness: forfeiting the game

A seventeen-year-old young man had lived in institutions for many years. He was not delinquent, mentally ill, unattractive, or stupid. He was the son of heroin-addicted parents. The irresponsibility of his long-lost parents had cost the boy years of suffering. When confronted about his need to forgive them, he was adamant. "You can't expect me to forgive them; it's too much. I'll never be able to do that!" He was right, but the fact remained. He could not heal or develop fully until he was willing to go far beyond normal expectations.

Nonforgiveness is easily defined: "I will not forgive" or in its more intense form, "I will never forgive." Some common variations of this are:

- "I will hate her 'til the day I die."
- "I will never forgive my father."
- "I can't (won't) forgive!"

Nonforgiveness inhibits healing and growth so effectively that it is not even in the ballpark with respect to the quest for getting better. Nobody bats a thousand, but no one has to bat zero either. Nonforgiveness is synonymous with forfeiting a game before it starts. Most of us cannot play full time in the majors, but we can show up in the ballpark. Even sandlot ball is better than not playing at all.

Unfortunately, forgiveness in one circumstance does not automatically assure forgiveness in another. For instance, forgiving a parent does not mean we forgive a spouse. They are separate issues. We may score a home run in the major league and strike out on the sandlot team in another. Relapses (slumps), of course, can beset us, tumbling us from the majors right out of the game.

Nonforgiveness comes in two forms. Specific nonforgiveness pertains to feelings toward a particular individual and related to one or more offense. Pervasive nonforgiveness is more inclusive and reflects a general unwillingness to practice forgiveness toward anyone. Pervasive nonforgiveness is the more serious. It effectively blocks all channels for emotional or spiritual healing and growth. Specific nonforgiveness allows for some development provided the bitterness is not so intense that it eclipses all hope for improvement.

A thirty-five-year-old man lived most of his life in bitterness because his father had inflicted such cruelty on him as a child. They lived in a remote area and no one was aware how sadistic his father had been. Savage beatings were his father's idea of Christian discipline. At age fourteen he hated both his father and God. In bitterness, he left home; he preferred to burn in hell rather than be subjected to further abuse. He felt no loss of love since he had never known love in the first place. He viewed his father as a tyrant and himself as a cheap source of farm labor. Determined nonforgiveness compounded his bitterness.

Although his father had been dead for years, his bitterness finally gave way to forgiveness. He began healing and grew into a caring, responsible father to his own children. One day he shared his feelings: "I figured if I can forgive my father, I can forgive anything that comes along."

Major league players make it look easy—the mark of a true professional. But most players work up through the leagues and reach the top only after years of struggle and self-discipline. Major league forgiveness is usually attained the same way. Most of us will never have a full-time career in the majors. But who knows until we are willing to try out for the team. When we are at the bottom the only way to go is up.

Pseudoforgiveness: a game of scrub

"I thought I had forgiven, but it really was not from my heart," stated a young woman recovering from rape. She was not being superficial. She simply had not taken a serious view of forgiveness until she realized she could not get better without it.

Pseudoforgiveness is easy to define but difficult to identify since counterfeit forms of forgiveness may appear genuine. Pseudoforgiveness can be defined as "I will forgive but ...." Add any qualifier that disqualifies forgiveness. The following are some examples:

- "I'll forgive but I'll never forget."
- "I'll forgive but make sure it never happens again."
- "I'll forgive but I pray God will make him suffer as much as I have."

Other forms of pseudoforgiveness mask bitterness and do not confront real emotions. Glossing over hurt only provides a facade for naked anger. For instance:

- "Don't worry about it; I'll get over it."
- "I don't let it bother me anymore."
- "I just plain don't give a damn."

Pseudoforgiveness is like "scrub," a game children play when there are not enough to make two teams. It looks much like baseball. The rules are similar but it is not the real game. There are no "scrub" leagues.

Pseudoforgiveness restricts healing and growth and can contribute to false appearances of piety. Condescending attitudes of moral superiority serve as good examples. Extreme violence and hatred complete with holy wars mark Christian history. Iran's Ayatollah Khomeini shocked the civilized world when he ordered the murder of author Salmon Rushdie for his novel, *The Satanic Verses,* which angered the Islamic world.

Pseudoforgiveness disguises bitterness, an infection that can fester at any time. Ironically, it masks hostility to make it look like a virtue.

Forgiveness must be a way of life that nurtures healing and growth.

When Frederick William I, king of Prussia (1713-40), was dying, his wife attempted to motivate him to resolve the hatred he had for his brother-in-law, George II of England. The king ordered her to write to her brother and tell him he was forgiven. "But," he said, "do not do it until I am dead."[4]

With that same attitude, sanctimonious people pray for their enemies with a sincere hope that God will "heap coals of fire on their heads." [5] Bertrand Russell summarized this type of deceit when he said, "The infliction of cruelty with a good conscience is a delight to moralists. That's why they invented hell."[6]

Pseudoforgiveness becomes so deceptive that we delude ourselves—and others. We try desperately to prove our emotional health only to find depression or anger erupting at unexpected times. This is not necessarily overt psychological dishonesty; it is an attempt to short-circuit our having to deal with the depths of hurt and anger. Bitterness thrives; healing and growth die.

Conditional forgiveness: trying out for the minors

With rage in her voice, a divorced mother of three screamed at her therapist: "What do you mean: forgive him? He owes me over $10,000 child support. I'll be damned if I'll forgive him until he's paid every last dime!" Unfortunately, her words were prophetic. He did not pay and she condemned herself to live in bitterness. Eventually, her hostility grew so intense that her oldest son ran away to live with his father.

Conditional forgiveness is easy to define and not particularly difficult to practice. Simply defined, conditional forgiveness is "I will forgive if (when) ..." Add whatever condition is expected of the offender:

- "I'll forgive if she says she is sorry."
- "I'll forgive if he pays for it."
- "I'll forgive when I get even."

Conditional forgiveness works at times. Unlike nonforgiveness or pseudoforgiveness which never works, conditional forgiveness can point toward the major leagues. At least it is a tryout.

A problem arises with conditional forgiveness, however, because inner peace is at the mercy of the offender. If he meets the conditions and we forgive, we get better. But the offender may not be interested in our conditions and not care at all about our suffering. In that case, anger stews into bitterness. We have struck out!

Conditional forgiveness has impressive precedents and is deeply ingrained in culture. In the biblical parable of the unforgiving servant, a man who was forgiven a debt of over $10 million refused to forgive a $20 debt another man owed him. When the lender who had forgiven the enormous debt learned of the servant's refusal to forgive the petty debt, he revoked his forgiveness and the servant was put into jail. The parable summarized the lesson this way: "So also my heavenly Father will do to everyone of you if you do not forgive your brother from your heart."[7]

The implication is that even divine forgiveness may have conditions. Self-imposed conditions were taught in the model prayer: "...and forgive us our debts as we also have forgiven our debtors ...."[8]

Certainly, forgiving others is an excellent exercise for receiving forgiveness. But the problem of conditions remains. True forgiveness is intimately personal and has nothing to do with the behavior of anyone else. Heinrich Heine (1797-1856) expressed the attitude of conditional forgiveness when he said, "We should forgive our enemies, but only after they have been hanged first." [9] Refusal to forgive when our conditions are not met renders healing and growth impotent. It's a washout!

Conditional forgiveness may be an effort to preserve dignity by attempting to control the uncontrollable. Of course, the thinking, the feeling, and the behavior of others is out of our control. Efforts to manipulate others by establishing conditions for forgiveness may indicate that the intent to forgive is less than sincere. A college senior said, "I don't want to be a goody-goody; it hasn't gotten me anywhere." Forgiveness builds its own dignity through healing and growth.

Forgiveness can be more difficult when we do not feel forgiven. Unforgiveness of others may intensify our own bitterness. In frustration, we may withhold forgiveness or attempt to negotiate more favorable conditions.

The actuality, of course, is that we do not control how others feel about us. We cannot force another person to forgive. We can only ask forgiveness and make amends when possible. This increases the probability of our being forgiven, but there are no guarantees. If another person refuses to forgive, that is his or her problem. A mature person can forgive regardless of whether forgiveness is or is not forthcoming.

Unconditional forgiveness: major league stardom

Major league ball players are important people. They are role models and command unbelievable salaries. When I was a boy, I met some honest-to-goodness stars. This was a special treat. I was not sure how their athletic accomplishments related to endorsements of beer, bubble gum, and razor blades, but it made no difference. They were major league!

Unconditional forgiveness is simple to define but extremely difficult to practice. The best definition I can formulate is "I forgive—regardless." There are no qualifications, distortions, or conditions. The following are some examples:

- "I forgive; it's over."
- "I forgive totally."
- "I forgive. Period."

Unconditional forgiveness is 24 karat. There are no pollutants to foul attitude, no infections to inhibit healing or growth. In an exciting article titled "Forgiveness: Love's Healing Miracle," Lewis B. Smedes gave this moving account:

> … one December day in 1983, Pope John Paul II walked into a dank cell of Rebibbia prison outside Rome to meet Mehmet Ali Agca, the man who had fired a bullet at his heart. In a quiet moment alone with his would-be assassin, the pope forgave him.
>
> For the ordinary person, however, forgiveness is not easy. It seems almost unnatural. Our sense of fairness tells us that people should pay for the wrong they do. But forgiving can bring a miraculous kind of healing—even reconciliation.[10]

Leaders like Pope John Paul II are important. They challenge us upward to major league, superstar performance. Fortunately, some of us can play a few innings and gain remarkable healing and growth in the process.

Unconditional forgiveness is a personal choice. With that choice, we regain control of our inner lives. On the other hand, we can choose to continue in bitterness, but the responsibility for doing so is solely ours. Even more important, we can also choose to get better.

Some eight years ago, a colleague consulted me about a young woman who had been horribly victimized. I suggested that unconditional forgiveness was a prerequisite for the girl's recovery. The therapist was skeptical, but she agreed to try. We corresponded regularly and three years after beginning treatment my colleague sent a stirring major league case vignette:

> The case came to the attention of authorities after a fifteen-year-old girl made repeated calls to police, hotlines, and mental health emergency numbers. She threatened to kill herself but refused to give her name or any other information. Eventually, the calls were traced and the young woman was brought to a professional therapist in a state of agitated psychotic confusion.
>
> Slowly, the girl began to unravel horrible experiences of rape. She told of being tied to her bed and having a knife inserted into her vagina. She sobbed as she recalled the pain and humiliation of relentless sexual exploitation.
>
> The patient was admitted to a local hospital where she made a serious suicide attempt, slashing her arms with broken glass. She was committed to a state hospital for intensive treatment.
>
> She identified her father as the rapist. He was arrested but never convicted. The girl was placed in a shelter and found refuge later with caring relatives.
>
> Therapeutic forgiveness was slow and agonizing. She loved her father but the scars on her arms served as reminders of her bitterness.
>
> The girl finally achieved a liberating level of forgiveness. She shared some personal insights with her therapist:
>
> "I held it against him for so long, but it didn't help. I can't be happy and sad at the same time.
>
> "The key to happiness is forgiveness. I had to put it in the past and go on with my life.
>
> "I believe God helped me. I didn't feel right until my heart was right.
>
> "I don't know if Dad has changed but forgiveness was for me.
>
> "I found strength helping another girl I met in the hospital. I understood how much she hurt."
>
> —*Anonymous, but willing to share.*

I have stayed in contact with my colleague. The young woman has become a well-adjusted adult. She must know the thrill of hitting a home run in the world series.

Unconditional forgiveness forfeits any reservations or qualifications. Offenders are not required to be sorry, ask forgiveness, change in any way, or even know they are forgiven. By conscious choice we are able to forgive without reservation. A great weight is lifted and we begin to heal and grow.

We see the epitome of unconditional forgiveness demonstrated centuries ago. It altered the entire course of human history. Under a blistering sun, Jesus of Nazareth was barbarously nailed to a cross and died in naked humiliation. [11] Gamblers rolled dice for his robe; his dignity was crushed. Most of all, he was the victim of cold-blooded, calculated slaughter. When one is robbed of life, all else pales into insignificance. No one can perpetrate a greater crime.

Yet, at the height of excruciating pain and depth of despair, he cried out, "Father, forgive them; they know not what they do." The absence of conditions and purity of forgiveness are strikingly clear. His forgiveness did not require the return of his robe, a change of heart among those cruel people, or that they spare his life.

Unconditional forgiveness shook the foundations of the earth. In the agony of death, he prayed intensely but simply, "Father, forgive them...."

May the blessings of healing and growth be yours as you undertake to forgive in the same way.

Conclusion

Conclusions usually summarize and reflect on the major points of a book. But this book is simply outlined; you can do that for yourself.

The only conclusions that really matter are: 1) your commitment to live as a forgiving person and 2) the distance you travel from bitterness to betterness. I suggest you pause to consider and jot down your personal conclusions. Perhaps someday you will share them with me.

Notes

Introduction

1. Robert Jay Lifton. *The Nazi Doctors: Medical Killing and the Psychology of Genocide* (New York: Basic Books, Inc.,1986), p. 5.
2. *Selma Times Journal,* Vol. 160, No. 225, February 18, 1988, p. 3.
3. *Selma Times Journal,* Vol. 161, No. 153, November 25, 1988, p. 5.
4. Bartlett, *Familiar Quotations,* 14th ed., 1968, p. 839.
5. C.S. Lewis. *Mere Christianity* (New York: The MacMillan Co., 1953), p. 89.

Chapter I

1. Albert Ellis, *Humanistic Psychotherapy: The Rational Emotive Approach* (New York: Julian Press, Inc., 1973), p. 37.
2. Thomas A. Harris, *I'm OK—You're OK: A Practical Guide to Transactional Analysis* (New York: Harper & Row Publishers, Inc., 1969), pp. 5-7.

Chapter II

1. Maxwell Maltz, *Psycho-cybernetics* (New York: Pocket Books, 1960), pp. 159-166.
2. Herbert L. Gravitz and Julie D. Bowden, *Guide to Recovery: A Book for Adult Children of Alcoholics* (Holmes Beach, Florida: Learning Publications, Inc., 1985), p. 64.

3. *Ibid.,* p. 21. Authors cite Claudia Black, *It Will Never Happen to Me* (Denver: Medical Administration Company, 1981).

4. *Ibid.,* p. 21.

5. Theodore Rubin, *The Angry Book* (New York: MacMillan Publishing Co., 1970). For full discussion see pp. 47ff.

6. Gravitz & Bowden, *Guide to Recovery*, p. 37.

7. Glenn Doman, *How to Teach Your Baby to Read: The Gentle Revolution Series* (Philadelphia: The Better Baby Press, 1979), pp. 2, 32-33.

Chapter III

1. Jesse Lair, *I Ain't Much Baby—But I'm All I've Got* (New York: Doubleday Co., Inc., 1969).

2. Lewis Grizzard, *They Tore Out My Heart and Stomped That Sucker Flat* (Atlanta: Peachtree Publishers, 1982).

3. Matthew 22: 34-40 (RSV).

Chapter IV

1. David Augsburger, *The Freedom of Forgiveness: Seventy Times Seven* (Chicago: Moody Press, 1970), p. 19.

2. *Ibid.,* p. 58. Author cites William C. Menninger, "Behind the Many Flaws of Society," *National Observer,* August 31, 1964, p. 18.

3. Doman, *How to Teach Your Baby to Read*, pp. 17-18.

4. Robert J. Ackerman, *Let Go and Grow: Recovery for Adult Children* (Pompano Beach, Florida: Health Communications, Inc., 1987).

5. Ruth 1:16-17 (RSV).

Chapter V

1. Stuart Berg Flexner. *I Hear America Talking* (New York: Van-Nostrand Rhinbold Co., 1976), p. 19.

2. Maltz, *Psycho-cybernetics,* p. 161.

3. Peter Mazuk *et al.* "Increased Risk of Suicide in Persons with AIDS," *Journal of the American Medical Association.* Vol. 259, No. 93, March 4, 1988, pp. 1333 ff.

4. Clifton Fadiman, ed., *The Little Brown Book of Anecdotes* (Boston: Little Brown and Co., 1985), p. 223.

5. Ref: Romans 12:20 (RSV).

6. Lawrence J. Peter, *Peter's Quotations: Ideas for Our Time* (New York: Bantam Books, 1977), p. 195.

7. Matthew 18:23-35 (RSV).

8. Matthew 6:12 (RSV).

9. Peter, *Peter's Quotations,* p. 197.

10. Lewis B. Smedes, "Forgiveness: Love's Healing Miracle," *Reader's Digest,* Vol. 127 (August, 1985), pp. 86-89.

11. Ref: Luke 23 (RSV).

Bibliography

Ackerman, Robert J. *Let Go and Grow: Recovery for Adult Children.* Pompano Beach, Florida: Health Communications, Inc., 1987.

Augsburger, David. *The Freedom of Forgiveness: Seventy Times Seven.* Chicago: Moody Press, 1970.

Ellis, Albert. *Humanistic Psychotherapy: The Rational Emotive Approach.* New York: Julian Press, Inc., 1973.

Doman, Glenn. *How to Teach Your Baby to Read: The Gentle Revolution Series.* Philadelphia: The Better Baby Press, 1979.

Fadiman, Clifton, ed. *The Little Brown Book of Anecdotes.* Boston: Little Brown and Co., 1985.

Flexner, Stuart Berg. *I Hear America Talking.* New York: Van Nostrand Rhinbold Co., 1976.

Gravitz, Herbert L. and Bowden, Julie D. *Guide to Recovery: A Book for Adult Children of Alcoholics.* Holmes Beach, Florida: Learning Publications, Inc., 1985.

Grizzard, Lewis. *They Tore Out My Heart and Stomped That Sucker Flat.* Atlanta: Peachtree Publishers, 1982.

Harris, Thomas A. *I'm OK—You're OK: A Practical Guide to Transactional Analysis.* New York: Harper & Row, 1969.

Lair, Jesse. *I Ain't Much Baby—But I'm All I've Got.* New York: Doubleday Co., Inc., 1969.

Lewis, C.S. *Mere Christianity.* New York: The MacMillan Co., 1953.

Lifton, Robert Jay. *The Nazi Doctors: Medical Killing and the Psychology of Genocide.* New York: Pocket Books, 1960.

Maltz, Maxwell. *Psycho-cybernetics.* New York: Pocket Books, 1960.

Mazuk, Peter *et al.* "Increased Risk of Suicide in Persons with AIDS." *Journal of the American Medical Association,* Vol. 259, No. 9, March 4, 1988. p. 1333ff.

Peter, Lawrence J. *Peter's Quotations: Ideas for Our Time.* New York: Bantam Books, 1977.

Rubin, Theodore. *The Angry Book.* New York: MacMillan Publishing Co., 1970.

Selma Times Journal. Selma, Alabama: Selma Newspaper, Inc., Vol. 161, No. 153, November 25, 1988.

Selma Times Journal, Selma, Alabama: Selma Newspaper, Inc., Vol. 160, No. 225, March 18, 1988.

Smedes, Lewis B., "Forgiveness: Love's Healing Miracle." *Reader's Digest,* Vol. 127, pp. 86-89, August,1985.